ABUELA IN SHADOW,
ABUELA IN LIGHT

LIVING OUT

Gay and Lesbian Autobiographies

DAVID BERGMAN, JOAN LARKIN, and RAPHAEL KADUSHIN
Founding Editors

ABUELA IN SHADOW,
ABUELA IN LIGHT

Rigoberto González

The University of Wisconsin Press

The University of Wisconsin Press
728 State Street, Suite 443
Madison, Wisconsin 53706
uwpress.wisc.edu

Gray's Inn House, 127 Clerkenwell Road
London ECIR 5DB, United Kingdom
eurospanbookstore.com

Printed in the United States of America
This book may be available in a digital edition.

Library of Congress Cataloging-in-Publication Data

Names: González, Rigoberto, author.
Title: Abuela in shadow, abuela in light / Rigoberto González.
Other titles: Living out.
Description: Madison, Wisconsin : The University of Wisconsin Press, [2022] |
Series: Living out: gay and lesbian autobiographies
Identifiers: LCCN 2021038697 | ISBN 9780299337605 (paperback)
Subjects: LCSH: González, Rigoberto—Family. | Grandmothers—Biography. |
Tarasco women—Biography.
Classification: LCC PS3557.04695 Z46 2022 | DDC 813/.54 [B]—dc23
LC record available at https://lccn.loc.gov/2021038697

¡Jikeni kánekua tsïpesïnga exeni, naná k'eri!

Contents

ABUELA IN SHADOW, ABUELA IN LIGHT

Unrest

Here you say—what? Grandmother? Over there they say abuela.
But we say naná k'eri. Or just nana.

—Abuela's lessons in Purépecha

LET'S WORK BACKWARD and begin at Abuela's grave.

I visited only once, in 2016, five years after Abuela's death. My friend Sandra and I took a drive down to visit her mother, who still resided in Thermal, California, where Sandra and I once lived as children. On the way back to Sandra's new home in Riverside, where we met as college students, she decided to stop by the Coachella Valley Public Cemetery to leave a bouquet of daisies and yellow roses for her father. It dawned on me that perhaps my grandparents were also buried there, in the only local cemetery either of us knew about. Abuelo died in 2008 and Abuela in 2011.

"Just walk into the office and ask," Sandra suggested.

I did, with no expectations, which is why I showed up empty-handed. Especially since I didn't remember the dates of their deaths in that moment. I only had their names. And how many Ramón Gonzálezes and María Carrillos were there in this mostly Mexican county? The Coachella Valley was 60 percent Latino. Its most recent prominent growth happened in the 1980s, when Peter W. Rodino, a congressman from New Jersey, pushed forward a number of immigration reforms and policies. We knew quite a few people, including those who had married into our family, who had benefited from them. These folks were affectionately called "Rodinos."

Finding my grandparents in this field of burials, however, turned out to be easier than I anticipated. Since they were buried together, there was only one match. When I asked how I could get to it, the woman at the office offered to drive me there in a golf cart.

As I climbed onto the passenger seat, I recalled the time I mentioned my half sisters to my friend Rich. When he asked me why I hadn't reached out all these years after our father's death, my lazy explanation was that I had no clue where to start. The truth was I didn't want to know or become entrenched with people who were blood relatives yet complete strangers.

"Try Facebook," Rich suggested.

I did. And less than two minutes later I came upon their personal pages. Still, I didn't try to communicate with them. I had nothing to say. With Abuela, on the other hand, there was much that I wanted to say. Or rather, I had been itching to sift through the rubble to recover the woman I had left behind.

The cemetery was nothing like the one in Michoacán my family was used to. At Panteón San Franciscano in the town of Zacapu, generations of both sides of my family were buried there, including my mother. As a child I visited during the Days of the Dead, and the cemetery turned into a colorful open-air living room decked in cempasúchil and lighted candles. Clusters of people sat around the tombstones and used the surfaces as tabletops. At the center: candy skulls, but also fruit, bread, and bottles of alcohol and soda. Each tomb was unique in style and size; thus, each scene was a personalized altar. The ones that appealed to me the most were the ones whose tall crosses were wrapped in strings of golden flowers. Suddenly there was joy, not somberness, at the sight of them. The old women in rebozos offered quiet prayer, but by late evening people broke out into spirited song, encouraged by the guitars that strummed their tunes from different parts of the community gathering.

Since I was still a child, I joined the other kids zigzagging along the paths, dodging graves and grown-ups, and until one of us collided with something (which usually shut down our raucous game of chase) we were free to scuttle like strays through the cemetery. The scent of cempasúchil was intoxicating. I felt my body elevate, as if I had stepped into dream. The surreal evening—a late-night family gathering among the graves—certainly affirmed that feeling. I was dizzy, and I was flying, and I was giddy with pleasure.

As the woman drove me through the symmetrical grid of the Coachella cemetery, I was taken aback at how cold and distant this final resting place seemed. It was just like the government housing I grew up in, the Fred Young Farm Labor Camp—or El Campo, as it was commonly known. With every structure similar to the ones lining the rest of the street, we knew which apartment was ours because we just knew how to get there. One year street names were posted, but I'm certain very few people bothered to learn them. They were so after-the-fact at that point and therefore useless. There was no individuality or character allowed by the housing office's many policies. Undeterred, my grandparents did wonders with the garden, growing a variety of flowers, herbs, and even a small papaya tree. It was quite an arresting sight, and the housing office didn't send a letter of complaint.

Eventually, the housing administrators gave up trying to keep everything uniform and actually encouraged the residents to beautify their gardens with a friendly competition. Cash award. Abuela was ready for this challenge and proceeded to work her magic. On every available bush, flowers sprouted: roses and chrysanthemums blossomed side by side—from the same stem! The small lemon tree with its thorny branches was ablaze with bright-red geraniums and orange dahlias. A vine with purple clementine flowers stretched from the corner of the window to the roof and along the roof's edge like a strip of Christmas lights. At night, the pistils would light up.

"Your grandmother was upset she got disqualified," Abuelo explained. "They were asking for real flowers, not the fake ones with the price tags still attached."

I almost let out a chuckle remembering that incident as we drove past the graves, which were nothing more than flat slabs pressed into the earth. Bouquets of flowers still wrapped in plastic were stuck into the small opening at the base of each surface. If there were no flowers, the holes looked like shower drains without covers. From a distance, the bouquets appeared isolated and awkward, as if socially distanced. In short, there was no character here.

When we finally stopped at the edge of one of the grassy fields, the woman pointed. "It'll be the third one on this row."

I marveled at how methodical and orderly this whole design was. At the panteón, graves and loved ones got lost. Abuela's two daughters Ramona and Verónica, who died in infancy, for example, were buried long ago, when the family could not even afford headstones. During one visit to Michoacán, when I was a teenager, Abuelo decided to look for them, and we never found them. We didn't think to visit the administration office, but I'm not sure if that would've helped. Soon he gave up with a short sigh and simply gestured with his arm. "Well, they're buried around this part."

He had better luck finding the graves of his parents, whom we affectionately referred to as Abuelo Pilar and Abuela Ramona. Abuelo Ramón was expressionless when he stood over the graves. Whatever was going through his head at that moment he kept to himself. I do remember how the bottom of his boot scraped the top of the tombstone as he kicked away debris that had dropped from the pine tree above.

That image popped into my head when I encountered his grave. It was difficult to wrap my brain around the fact that both he and Abuela were buried there. The ebony plaque on the grave had pronounced lettering spelling out GONZALEZ. Below that, RAMON and MARIA, with their respective birth and death dates. But only Abuelo's face was staring out from the plaque. Abuela's image had not been added, five years after her burial. The light in that side of the room had not been switched on. She was asleep in the dark.

Suddenly I became indignant. This wasn't where Abuela wanted to end up. Not in this emotionless cemetery and certainly not side by side with Abuelo, whose name had taken precedence over hers. She was María Carrillo, not María González. This is not who she was and where she belonged. It was an obscene final blow to her dignity. But as her grandson I had no say in the matter, not when Tía Melania, Abuela's only living daughter, had taken control of Abuela's life and finances in the final years of her life. I had not spoken to my aunt since I left for college in 1988.

It was because of this estrangement that I was not told of Abuela's death. Nor had I been invited to the funeral, even though my brother and I had lived with our grandparents through most of our adolescence. I only found out about her passing because one of the cousins was instant messaging with my brother, Alex, on Facebook and he let it slip.

"When did she die?" I asked Alex when he told me about the exchange. "Last month," he said.

My brother had called me from Mexicali, across the U.S.-México border. I was at Yaddo, a writer's residency in Saratoga Springs, New York.

"And why was this kept from us?"

"I asked the same thing."

"And what did he say?" I pressed on.

"He said, 'Well, you know how it is.'"

And I understood very well what that meant. Once upon a time, all nineteen of us slept under one roof, an experiment in communal living that shattered as petty conflicts and long-held grudges surfaced. And then there were those egregious acts committed in secret. How could we face one another after all that?

Over the years, when I spoke about Abuela to friends, I always began with a caveat: she's not the typical Mexican grandmother. Some would say the same about theirs, or they would balk: "Who *is*?" Yet I still saw my grandmother as one of a kind—a woman who challenged the depictions of those matronly, domestic older ladies we watched on Mexican telenovelas, las abuelitas. Abuelitas loved unconditionally; they doted over their grandchildren and indulged the rebellious ones who gave their parents grief. They protected the vulnerable and wept when any family members experienced distress. But how elated they became when anyone they loved received good luck or good news. Their gentle souls were mirrored in the care they took in arranging flowers in a vase, in stirring the stew in the pot, in listening to the others bring news from the outside because abuelitas had no reason to venture beyond the walls of the house. Their place was in the well-lighted living rooms, the TV or the record player at low volume as they waited patiently for the next person to walk in so that they could come alive again.

I knew not to trust those staged versions of grandmothers, but they were irresistible. Desirable. And although I had learned to accept Abuela for who she was, I couldn't shake this feeling that I longed for the type of grandmother she wasn't. Perhaps that grandmother might have offered something different, something to make being the gay grandson in the González family more bearable. Perhaps I could have forgiven such a grandmother more readily. I still had mixed feelings about Abuela María.

One day, I was looking through my grandparents' dresser for a comb. Since Abuelo cut my hair, I knew he had a supply stashed somewhere. When I opened a bottom drawer, I came across cassette tapes, many of them old recordings of Purépecha bands playing pirekuas. Abuelo enjoyed hearing the violins and guitar in the truck whenever we drove to Michoacán. His idea of setting the mood.

Among the dusty cassette tapes, I found a few blank ones. Tío Ramón used them to transfer Abuelo's vinyl records, expanding Abuelo's travel music selection. I became intrigued when I saw one labeled El Rancho, which was where Abuelo owned a lot with an old three-bedroom house. There was no running water, no telephone line, but there was electricity. When we visited Tía Melania in Mexicali, we would go to El Rancho for cookouts and other family gatherings.

I played the tape on Tío Ramón's boom box and became pleasantly surprised that this was an impromptu recording of one of those family get-togethers. The adults were tipsy. Every once in a while, one of my cousins could be heard in the background, whining or laughing. I became curious about how this recording came to be because Tío Ramón, the technology guru, wasn't present in the recording. Perhaps one of my older cousins was the culprit. A joke taping that suddenly became valuable enough for Abuelo to preserve.

In the recording, there was the usual teasing and banter between my father and Tío Rafa, and then Tía Melania's contagious laughter consumed the room. But then came the highlight of the moment—the adults began to reminisce with song. Abuelo, encouraged by my father's wingman antics, sang snippets of his sentimental favorites. Then Tía Melania sang a few notes. Then my father. Then my uncle. I was shocked to hear my mother and my uncle's wife partaking in a clunky duet. Everyone had joined in the fun. Except Abuela. I heard her soft voice chiming in with commentary on occasion, but she didn't sing, not even after her children tried to coax her into it. Abuela didn't sing. In fact, I couldn't recall hearing my grandmother break into spontaneous song the way Abuelo did. Whenever he did so, Abuela looked over at me and started to giggle.

On those Mexican telenovelas, las abuelitas sang while doing household chores like folding laundry and handwashing the dishes. They sang while they knit. Most importantly, they sang to their grandchildren—comforting lullabies that eased them into the calm of sleep. I never heard my grandmother sing.

My friend Sandra came up behind me. "Hey," she said. "Did you find them?"

That question lingered in the air.

Sandra took one quick look at the stone slab, at Abuelo posing in a suit, an outfit I never got to see him wear. She added, "Your grandma's missing."

She was, I concluded. I would have to begin my search.

Abuela's Photographs

Here you say house. Over there they say casa. But we say
k'umánchikua.

—Abuela's lessons in Purépecha

I DON'T HAVE A SINGLE PHOTOGRAPH of Abuela María in her later years,
though I know they exist. There was one in particular that amused me. It
was of my two grandmothers dancing together on the dirt surface patio of
El Rancho, the property in Mexicali where Abuelo, my father, Tío Rafa,
and my brother, Alex, would eventually build homes, one right next to
the other. El Rancho was the gathering place because there was more freedom there, despite the lack of plumbing and the nerve-wracking outhouse.
But in 1981, the year that photograph was taken, there was only one house
standing in that vast lot of land. The water canal running across the entire
neighborhood had yet to be paved over, allowing for a proper asphalt street.

The occasion for the party was Abuela Herminia's arrival from Zacapu.
She had come at the bidding of my mother, who wanted Abuela Herminia
nearby to help out with the cooking and caring for my brother and me. My
mother's health had been declining quickly. Heart surgery was in her future.

Abuela Herminia rode the bus all the way to Mexicali. She would stay
in El Rancho, in that run-down house once owned by Tía Melania's husband, until permission was granted to cross the border and stay with my
mother for a short period of time. To make her feel welcome, my father and
Abuelo Ramón made birria in a large pot over a brazero. Abuela Herminia
came bearing gifts of her own: a small cluster of blue and red mazorcas,
which pleased Abuelo to no end. I don't recall what he did with them, but

for the next few days they were tied to the kitchen window so that the kernels could sparkle like sapphires and rubies in the sun.

My father, ever the instigator, decided to play music on the radio at high volume. After my grandmothers had a few beers in them, it wasn't too difficult to convince them to dance despite the ninety-degree summer heat.

Abuela María had a bandanna tied around her head. She wore pants, like always, and a pair of sandals. Abuela Herminia sported her usual look: a knee-length skirt and pantyhose, and a pair of black canvas shoes. If it weren't for the beer in her hand, people might have mistaken her for a nun.

My father commemorated that day by taking picture after picture of the two women dancing, of Abuelo stirring the pot of birria, and of my brother and me watching our grandmothers with amusement from a distance. My mother was laid out in bed back in California, looked after by one of my aunts.

I wondered if it had been for my mother's benefit that my father had taken those photographs. Perhaps as evidence that the two families could get along, particularly during this difficult time. It was common knowledge that Abuelo Ramón thought very little of Abuela Herminia, and vice versa. Their clashes were legendary.

"I can take care of the grandchildren better than you can," he once proclaimed. "I have money to give them. They'll never go hungry in my house, unlike yours."

"Well, I may not be able to give them money," Abuela Herminia retorted. "But I can give them love. That's something you've never given anyone in your entire life!"

"I can offer them love too," Abuelo protested.

"Well, where do you keep it, behind your balls? Because I have yet to see you offer any of it. Even to your woman."

Abuelo Ramón and Abuela Herminia were very similar in temperament: they became angry quite quickly and weren't afraid to open their mouths. Abuela María and Abuelo Melecio, on the other hand, didn't engage in conflict, and simply watched the run-ins from a safe distance, expressionless.

Those photographs documented an unlikely truce between Abuelo Ramón and Abuela Herminia. I must have looked at the pictures often because I still remember that day clearly. I too recognized the significance of seeing Abuelo Ramón and Abuela Herminia content for once, in the same place at the same time.

After my parents passed away, all those photographs vanished, inherited by someone other than Alex and me. It wasn't until my visit to Michoacán, nearly forty years later, that one of my uncles pointed out that they had found a photo album belonging to my mother, and that the family agreed that I had a right to claim it.

"I mean," Tío Chuy added, "what's going to happen when the rest of your mother's siblings die? Our children never knew your mother. These photographs will mean nothing to them."

The album dated back to the late 1960s and into the '70s. The psychedelic design on the cover was of that era, with green-petaled flowers melting into a sea of red and orange. I called my brother immediately, since we had always bemoaned the fact that we had very few of our parents' belongings.

"It's got pictures of us as babies in Delano," I said with excitement. My brother and I had been born in Bakersfield in the early '70s, but our parents settled in Delano and later Lamont, two farm-working communities in Central California, before returning to Michoacán when Alex and I were toddlers.

"There are pictures of our baptisms," I continued. "As well as our baptism certificates. The names of my godparents are Primitivo and Rebeca Mendiola."

"What about mine?" he asked.

"Yours are Abuelo Ramón and Abuela María."

I leafed through the entire album with my brother on the line. I found color photos of my parents when they were dating, and after they were newly married. My mother posed with me sitting on a car hood, her second pregnancy quite prominent. Since our family picked grapes for a living, they were also involved in the grape boycotts of the '60s and '70s. Someone thought to document the marches and strikes. In a few of these pictures, Alex and I are part of the protest, me holding the UFW union flag. Abuela is holding my hand in one shot. In another, my mother is holding Alex and I'm pressed against her body.

There were also black-and-white photos of my mother and Abuela posing on the living room floor, a TV in the background. Neither of them is smiling. In fact, my mother looks rather despondent. My father, on the other hand, is all teeth in a picture of his lithe body on the floor, leaning on his right elbow as he places his left hand over my torso. I match his smile, looking happy and innocent. Clearly there were stories behind this series of photographs I would never get to know.

This photo album was the most substantial heirloom we would ever get to have from my mother. And I promised my brother I would hold on to it until it was time to bequeath it to his children.

"But you have to tell them about it," I said. "Tell them who these people are in the photographs, otherwise they will not appreciate them. These are family memories. If they are forgotten, then everyone in here truly dies."

I didn't mean to sound melodramatic, but that was a stark reality. Memories vanished and got lost. I recalled the many visits to the flea markets or antique shops. Invariably there was a bin filled with old photographs and family portraits, now relegated to vintage status. But at one time they were sacred, valued by those who knew about the lives of those pictured. Before strangers at shops thumbed through them without emotional connection, loved ones passed them around in kitchens and living rooms, punctuating their responses with bursts of delight or terms of endearment. I wanted this album to mean something for a bit longer, before it was cast aside as a record of the past that no one living could speak for.

The album also contained small black-and-white pictures taken in a portrait studio. All Mexican families had to have them because these were the obligatory photographs that ended up glued on important documents like diplomas, certificates, and passports. Any extras ended up in the family albums. My mother's album kept a few: of my father in his early twenties; of my grandfather, likely in his thirties; and two of my mother's brothers as teenagers. But the one that stood out was of Abuela María, long before she became a grandmother.

María Carrillo was likely in her late twenties or early thirties. She had given birth to her three oldest children, all under ten: Rigoberto, Melania, and Rafael. And perhaps baby Ramón, born in 1958, was crawling around already. Her hair was short and combed back, a hairstyle that she kept until the day of her death. Her sisters, Juana and Guadalupe, would also favor this look.

"Braids are for Indians," her husband once declared. María was Indigenous. A Purépecha. (Mexicans also used the word Tarasco, but, in general, Purépechas themselves did not.) Her dark skin, pronounced nose, and small eyes were all common Purépecha features.

She is elegant in this portrait taken at Fotos Sandoval in Mexicali. The business logo is stamped just underneath her image. Her earrings cling like small icicles to her lobes. The white blouse offers a striking contrast to her smooth, dark skin. But the pendant is hard to make out. The photographer took great care to include it in the portrait, cutting off the shot just below the piece of jewelry. It's either a cross or a dove. If it looks white, it's because the blouse underneath shows through the openings in the pendant.

María's expression is serious. It's the same look I will see in every other photograph of her taken over the decades. She's never smiling in any of them, belying her love of a good laugh. Picking up the cat and making it dance made her giggle. Watching people trip or drop something sent her into fits of laughter. And she was never one to pass up watching the antics of her favorite slapstick comedy movies starring Cantinflas, Tin Tan, Resortes, Viruta y Capulina, and of course, La India María. She and Abuelo would roar with each silly movement on the screen. Her humor was not malicious. She simply liked to be tickled.

Once, when we were living at El Campo, Tía Melania came by with her first grandson, who must have been five years old at that time. The visit was just like any other, cordial and brief. The young boy sported a bowl cut that amused Abuela, but nothing prepared her for the back of the boy's head. I had seen that modern cut—buzzed high and tight—many times. But Abuela hadn't. When the boy turned around, Abuela let out a shriek, followed by her trademark hiccup-like laugh. Worse yet, she pointed, as if inviting the rest of us to join in.

"Ay, Amá," Tía Melania said, exasperated.

The young boy knew he was the source of the joke. He pressed his body against his grandmother for protection. When he looked at me, I smiled unconvincingly. Abuela was in a zone all by herself and there was nothing we could do to snap her out of it.

"What do you have there?" I asked, hoping to distract him.

He looked at the toy in his hand, but then he made the mistake of turning his back to his great-grandmother, exposing the back of his buzzed head all over again. Abuela shrieked some more.

Despite those album photographs that showed a solemn woman, Abuela did find occasion to have some fun. She also enjoyed watching boxing and car racing on TV. And she didn't like to miss her telenovelas in the evening, while sipping on a cup of tea.

"Perrillo!" she called to Abuelo by his nickname, followed by the telenovela's title: "*Pobre señorita Limantour!*"

That's all Abuelo needed to hear to rush back to the couch, beside her.

I sometimes watched from the dining table, which had a chair that faced the TV because only two or three bodies could fit on the couch at one time. If we watched something together, I usually sat on the floor. But the chair was more like a place to wait for them to go to bed so that I could watch my own favorite shows on the American channels.

If Abuela and Abuelo had photo albums, they never shared them with me. In fact, I can't recall ever seeing pictures of the people on Abuela's side of the family. The cynic in me believes that Abuelo didn't allow it. Just like he didn't allow Abuela to travel to México when her parents died. Mamá Lola and Papá Juan, as they were affectionately called, were buried without Abuela present. News of their deaths, years apart, were two of the few times I saw my grandmother cry.

After Abuela's mother died, Tío Ramón, the youngest son, still lived at home because he was a bachelor. He approached Alex and me as we sat in our bedroom, watching cartoons.

"Do you see what a horrible person your grandfather is?"

I looked at him in surprise, suddenly aware that something grave was about to be shared.

"He's too damn cheap to let her go to Zacapu. He never liked my mom's family anyway."

"I don't get it," I said. "Why does he hate them?" I was keenly aware that he had no love for my mother's family either.

"Because they see what kind of man he is: cruel and vindictive."

"Then why did she marry him?" I asked.

Tío Ramón looked toward the TV. His eyes had glossed over. His face was still, reflecting the changing colors of light emanating from the screen. I would not get an answer to that question in that moment. I let it die in the air as I too turned to the TV. We were watching *The Peanuts*. Lucy was about to trick Charlie Brown into attempting to kick the football again. When she pulled the football back and Charlie Brown spun in the air, none of us laughed. This was a first. We always laughed together at that gag. In the living room, Tía Melania and my father were consoling Abuela. Abuelo had gone to hide in his room.

I got to see Mamá Lola and Papá Juan enough times to remember them. She was small and frail, wearing her striped rebozo as she watched over something cooking over a brazero. He wore thick glasses because his eyesight had been damaged after years of staring into the clay oven, watching over the bread that he sold at his tiny bakery.

I can only recall one significant interaction with Papá Juan. It took place during one of my solo visits to Michoacán, when I was committed to seeing as many of my relatives as I could. Papá Juan was living with Tía Juana, and it was she who encouraged me to spend a little time with the family patriarch who was not long for this world.

Papá Juan stood in the middle of the enclosed courtyard, watching over the youngest great-grandchildren. Two of his daughters and his only son all lived in the neighborhood, thus, he became a de facto babysitter for their grandchildren. Any house I entered was noisy with kids running about, and this was one way that Tía Juana could give Papá Juan something to do. He took the task seriously, warning a child about not climbing too high on that tree and reprimanding another for striking a plastic bowl until it cracked against the cement washboard.

"Bendición, Papá Juan," I said, bowing my head for his blessing.

"Whose child are you?" he asked after making the sign of the cross over me.

"Rigoberto's. The oldest son of María," I said.

He stared at me until the connection finally clicked.

"Ah, yes," he said. "How is your father? How is you grandmother?"

I offered him updates and also mentioned my grandmother's other children: Tío Rafa and Melos—what he affectionately called Tía Melania, and who was his favorite, according to her. "He always woke me up before he opened the bakery," she offered as evidence, "and would promise me my own special cinnamon bun topped with burnt sugar."

He asked about other relatives now living in the U.S. that I had not met or heard of. When I told him as much, he became emotional.

"You all leave and then scatter," he said. His voice cracked. "I wake up every morning to send you blessings and turn to the north, and then to the east. And then I find myself spinning around and around like a crazy man, throwing prayers to the wind because I have no idea where to turn to next."

I looked toward Tía Juana for direction. I was uncertain about how to respond to his shaky voice and tearful eyes. He pulled out a handkerchief from his pocket, blew his nose, and walked away slowly. Tía Juana smiled apologetically, signaling to me not to take it too personally because Papá Juan was an old man who had lived to see dozens of his great-grandchildren, and that this was likely the last time I would see him alive.

This good man had fathered a good woman who then married an awful man. It didn't make sense to me. Which is why I still long for those photographs of my two grandmothers dancing together. Abuela María was smiling, the only photograph I recall where she did so. Which made me wonder what was going through her mind in all the other photographs in which she wasn't.

Sanctuary

Over there they say mariposa. We say parákata. What do you say here? Butterfly. Pues, parákata.

—Abuela's lessons in Purépecha

María Carrillo was born in Nahuatzen, Michoacán, in 1929. She was four foot eleven. She was a full-blooded Purépecha, something my father never let his sons forget. "You have Purépecha blood in you," he told us.

As a teenager, I was already holding on tightly to my identity as a Mexican, ever since my family migrated to California in 1980. I was born in the U.S. and reared in Michoacán, but I couldn't simply slip back into an American self. I was not American like the children around me who spoke English as fluently as the American singers they listened to. My México, however, was also removed from my Purépecha roots, because I only spoke Spanish and was raised in the sprawling town of Zacapu, the center of the Purépecha empire, whose Indigenous communities had been pushed to the edges of the town. At Mercado Morelos, when the Purépecha women came down to sell prickly pears and bags of diced cactus leaves, Tío Catarino, my mother's brother, would gesture toward them with his chin and say mockingly, "Look, the people of your grandmother, la uáhri." Annoyed, I distanced myself from them.

"Uáhri also means princess," my father explained once. "Your grandmother is a princess."

But that didn't do much to appease my anxiety that I was somehow associated with the small dark women in long braids and colorful dresses who were treated so shabbily by their Mexican customers. What enraged me the most was when people tried to bargain the women's prices down, prices that were already bargains in my eyes. It was an outlandish disregard for the labor of picking prickly pears and cleaning cactus leaves, not to mention the long hours of sitting on the cold mercado floor. Well-dressed ladies were the worst clients, justifying their meager offers by deriding the quality of the product. Once I saw a Purépecha woman push back, and it was quite the scene. The client stormed off but not before the seller yelled out, "Eat churro!" It was satisfying to witness. But not until I matured did I feel a kinship with these women, who resembled my grandmother.

Abuela didn't talk much about being Purépecha, and certainly not in front of Abuelo. Throughout the years that I lived with them after my mother's death, I picked up a word or a detail here and there.

"Ichúskuta," she once said, holding up a tortilla.

Alex and I giggled as she placed the warm tortilla in the center of the breakfast table. These few minutes before the school bus arrived were one of the few times the three of us were alone. Abuelo tended to his garden or puttered around his truck, waiting for us to leave.

Abuela pointed to the flower decorating her coffee cup and proclaimed, "Tsïtsïki, which means flor in Spanish. What do they say here?"

"Flower," we said.

Decades later, I ponder her teaching method. She would make it a point to pronounce the word in three languages: English, which was "here"; Spanish, which was "over there"; and Purépecha, which was "us." We were three different tongues, even though the world insisted on keeping them apart.

I was reminded of just how Purépecha Abuela was when I traveled to Morelia, the capital of Michoacán, on my own in 2017, when I went to visit my mother's parents.

I had let fifteen years lapse before returning to Michoacán. The last time I had seen Abuela Herminia and Abuelo Melecio, I was thirty; my alcoholic father was still around then and still pleading for money. I was still saying no. I made the decision to visit despite a serious trepidation. The rumors about kidnappings in México by inept thugs were rampant. Anyone known to have relatives living in the U.S. became vulnerable.

"They'll kidnap your grandmother for thirty dollars," people said. "They'll return her without her thumbs, if they return her at all."

I didn't want to endanger Abuela Herminia's thumbs or any other part of her. But the detail of the torture got to me. Abuela was a master knitter, and she would sit in front of the house all afternoon with the needles in her hands, making doilies and table runners. To take that from her was a crueler fate than even the kidnappers imagined. I had stayed away, believing that by doing so I was keeping her safe.

As time passed, it became easier to choose other destinations for my summer travels. I flew to different states in México, like Oaxaca and Cuernavaca. I flew to Europe, to South America, and countless times I walked the historic streets of Old San Juan, where I became such a seasonal presence that the islanders thought I had relatives in the area.

When I bought a plane ticket to the newly built airport in Zinapécuaro, just outside Morelia, the stories of the crimes committed in the small towns of Michoacán had not subsided, as the drug cartels competed for control of land and resources.

Long ago, my mother's side of the family lost access to their cornfield up in the mountains. The corn industry was failing because it was cheaper for México to buy the crop from Iowa. Enterprising criminals began to cultivate marijuana instead. They needed everyone's fertile soil. And they took it.

If anyone asked why I was willing to take that risk, I offered the failsafe explanation that my grandparents were aging, that I didn't know how many years they had left, and that I was doing this to honor my mother's wishes to stay in touch with her parents. That was only partly true. What finally made me transcend this fear of going home were the devastating news articles about the monarch butterfly. A deadly combination of climate change and illegal logging was decreasing their numbers exponentially. What was once a spectacular sight to behold, as the monarchs descended into the forests of their ancestors, was now a natural phenomenon whose days were numbered. Or so the headlines foretold.

The monarch is the perfect metaphor for the González family's migration from México to the U.S. and then back again. We relocated from one country to the next, every other generation. My great-grandfather and father were Mexican citizens. My grandfather and I were U.S.-born. I had adopted the monarch as a symbol of my sexuality as well, since mariposa, the Spanish word for butterfly, was slang for homosexual. Its decimation forecasted, I knew I had to see the migration once again before it was too late. Demise was imminent for my two sentimental connections to Michoacán.

I had witnessed the magic of the migration once before, when I was a child growing up in Zacapu. Since my family were people of the mountain, scaling up on the weekends to check up on the cornfield, to hunt, to dig for medicinal roots, and to socialize with other families, we were not afraid of the arduous trek up to Angangueo, where the monarch butterfly biosphere is located, just a three-hour drive east of our town.

As a mischievous child, I learned the hard way about respect for nature during that family trek. When we finally reached the site, the butterflies were fluttering all around us, and it seemed like such an easy thing to pick up a branch and start swatting. I set into the insects with glee, until Abuelo Melecio took the switch from my hand and let me have it, the only time he ever punished me. I was more stunned by the fact that it had been him and not Abuela Herminia, who was the short-tempered one. I knew then I had committed some grave infraction and vowed never to do it again. Not because I would meet the same fate but because I had offended Abuelo Melecio. Abuelo was a good man. Even as a child I recognized this. He was a good man who liked good things, like horses, firewood, prayer, and butterflies.

I was now a middle-aged man in recovery after an extended illness that kept me walking with a cane for seven years. I no longer used the cane, but physical exercise was still a chore. None of this mattered. My mind was made up. I was going down to Michoacán to greet the monarchs.

November was the key month. The monarchs always arrived during the Days of the Dead, which only underscored the myth that these were the souls of our departed returning home. I had lost my father by then, and his parents, and a few cousins. Would they be among the kaleidoscope? It was already one week past the festivities, but the cemeteries were still alight with dry marigolds, including the one in Zacapu, where my mother was buried. In my family, it is tradition to pay our respects to the dead first. The taxi dropped me off in front of the entrance, and I zigzagged my way through the tombs to place my hand on the blue tile of my mother's resting place. I uttered the words, "I'm here."

After a quick visit, I walked up the road to my grandparents' house and was pleasantly surprised to find them sitting outside. Abuela fidgeted with her rebozo. No knitting needles.

"Good afternoon," I called out.

"Good afternoon," they answered. And I realized then that they didn't recognize me. It had been fifteen years since my last visit, but I hadn't changed dramatically. I was older, a little heavier, but I was still me, their first grandson.

"Do you know who I am?" I asked.

My grandmother narrowed her eyes. "No, I don't. Who are you?"

"I'm your grandson," I said. "I'm Avelina's son."

"And who is she?" Abuela said.

My heart sank. If I was fifteen years older, so were they. That meant Abuela was now in her eighties, and Abuelo in his nineties, the stage of life when memory fades. Their hair was completely white, and their faces had softened. Abuelo used crutches to move about. Tío Chuy and his wife had become their caretakers. They welcomed me and explained the hard truth: both my grandparents suffered from dementia.

When they asked me why I had not come any sooner, I confessed to them that I was afraid of one of my loved ones getting kidnapped.

"Oh, that doesn't happen very often," Tío Chuy reassured me. "And the bodies they find around here, they are not anyone we know. They are people dumped here from somewhere else."

At lunch, Abuelo started telling me about the time he fell off his horse. It was a story he would repeat two more times before I said good-bye again. Abuela would suddenly remember me, but minutes later she would forget. The sad cycle of light and dark was too much for me to bear. I kept my visit brief, promising to return soon. As I walked away, I heard Abuela ask Abuelo, "Who was that?" and Abuelo answered, "I'm not sure."

I took photographs and video footage of them speaking now that I had a phone with such capabilities. Fifteen years ago, this was unthinkable.

But the technology had come too late, or rather, I had returned too late with the technology. What was I taking back with me but images that captured a fraction of their long and beautiful lives?

I left Zacapu, which had not grown much over the years, and checked into a hotel in Morelia, the state capital. The city was more my pace, with its crowded streets and tourist traps. In my youth, my family refused to come to Morelia, except for special occasions like weddings, funerals, and graduations. They said the city was full of dangers and sin. The city was also full of people who, like my father, were descendants of the Purépecha. I kept being startled each time I bumped into a man who shared my father's Indigenous features.

My clothing singled me out as a tourist, which made me resentful because I had roots deep in the city's history. In nearby San Agustín, a former convent that was once a commercial center, my family kept a food stand for generations, selling corundas, a regional specialty, since the end of the Mexican Revolution, one century ago.

But I was determined not to be distracted. I went up to a kiosk next to the cathedral, where tours to the Rosario butterfly sanctuary were booked. And I was met with another devastating blow: the butterflies had not arrived.

"Not arrived?" I exclaimed. "How can that be? It's the middle of the month!"

The young woman shrugged her shoulders. "I don't know what else to tell you, mister. We're as shocked as anybody. But we hope that any day now, they will surprise us."

I beat myself up over my self-imposed exile. I had come too late to find my grandparents still lucid and I had come too late to find the butterfly migration still vibrant and healthy. Despite all this, I made the best of my visit, traveling to nearby towns I had not seen since my childhood. In Quiroga I ate all my favorites like carnitas and atole de grano. In Tzintzuntzan I visited the cemetery because I had relatives there, though I didn't know how to locate their graves. I also traveled to Pátzcuaro, to find that special needlework it was famous for, the kind Abuela Herminia also knew but rarely practiced because of her failing eyesight. She preferred to knit, not stitch.

Abuela María wasn't a practitioner of these arts. She could stitch a sock or a tear in our clothes, but we were always amused by her choice of thread.

"Green on brown," Tío Ramón announced as he showed us her handiwork on a pair of his pants. "I guess this way I'll never forget where the hole was."

In fact, Abuela didn't have an affinity to domestic chores, particularly in the kitchen. When, as a middle-aged man, I went to see my doctor, I was surprised that he suggested I eat Jell-O after I complained about my knees.

"I said my knees, not my teeth," I clarified.

"Yes, for your knees. Jell-O's good for your bones, tendons, and ligaments."

"But I can't stand Jell-O," I said. "It's too sweet."

"Sweet? What kind of Jell-O did you eat as a kid?"

Skeptical, I made Jell-O and discovered that it was tasty. I realized then that Abuela had added sugar to the mix, turning me off from consuming it again until my doctor's recommendation. There was a second item she cooked that made us fret: pancakes. We just couldn't get used to the powdery center of her version.

I missed Abuela María greatly, but not her cooking skills. As I traveled through the small towns, however, I could hear her speaking through the Purépecha vendors and small children who, for a few pesos in change, would sing a song that mixed Purépecha and Spanish. Abuela didn't get to teach us complete phrases, only the simple vocabulary of colors, animals, and numbers—tiny fragments of a culture that I could keep in my pocket and take wherever I went.

I had tried on a few occasions to meet my Purépecha relatives, but the generation that knew about Abuela, her journey to the U.S., and her crew of grandchildren that had been born American citizens had all passed away. By the time I went knocking on the doors of the tiny houses within a stone's throw of el lago de Pátzcuaro or along the cobblestone streets of Tzintzuntan, I was received with suspicion, which turned to curiosity that faded rapidly. No one wanted to entertain this distant relative who had not been mentioned before but who had come from the north offering nothing but questions. People were busy with jobs and school and life. Out of politeness, one woman—an older cousin I had been told about by an aunt in Zacapu—offered me a glass of water at the entrance of her house, then enlisted one of her little ones to translate since he was the Spanish speaker.

"My mother wants me to show you around," a boy named Miguel informed me as he led me by the hand away from the house and toward the town square. I tried to catch a glimpse over my cousin's shoulder of the photographs on the wall, but nothing caught my eye.

"How old are you, Miguel?" I asked.

"Six," he said.

My six-year-old tour guide took me directly to the ice cream shop, which was my cue to buy him a treat. Afterward we visited a mango seller preparing the fruit from the cart—another treat!—and finally settled on a stone bench. I couldn't imagine asking Miguel about our shared family history, so I settled for small talk.

"Your parents must be proud of you," I said. "You're so young and can speak two languages."

Miguel shrugged his shoulders. "We can all speak two languages," he said.

I realized then that my relatives' refusal to speak to me in Spanish was their way of keeping me at arm's length. They had no time for me. The sting of that moment convinced me to stop making unexpected visits.

"The best way to get to know them is at parties," my aunt said to me when I gave her the disappointing news that I had found no one to talk to me about Abuela. "Come down during the holidays and I'll take you down there myself."

That day would never come, because my aunt died soon after I left Michoacán. An embolism. The same affliction that her sister, my mother, had suffered. I had waited too long to search. And all those years I hadn't been searching, my family's memories and stories had been sinking deeper into the cemetery soil.

The second time I tried to talk to my Purépecha relatives, it was at Mercado Morelos. It turned out that Tío Catarino was telling the truth. Those women sitting on the floor, selling warm tortillas and peeled prickly pears, *were* my relatives. At my bidding, he took me to meet one of them. He introduced me as her cousin.

My Purépecha cousin, who was also named María, shook my hand but stayed seated, which made me feel awkward as I remained bent over her in order to hear her above the background noise.

"Náre chúsku," I said, offering what little I knew about greetings in Purépecha.

My cousin María, a woman in her mid-thirties, smiled with amusement and offered me a prickly pear that glowed like a magenta bulb in that market of dirty white tile and scuffed metal.

"Take it and don't offer to pay for it or you'll offend her," my uncle whispered in my ear.

I became nervous all of a sudden. This was the most inopportune moment to ask any questions, let alone invite myself to her house for an interview. Tío Catarino sensed my hesitation and jumped in.

"He wants to know about his family," he said. "About his Abuela María, from Nahuatzen."

My cousin turned and mumbled a phrase in Purépecha to the woman sitting beside her, who chuckled.

"Nahuatzen," she said. "What for? No jobs in Nahuatzen. Only hunger."

I wasn't sure if she had misunderstood or if we were in fact on such divergent wavelengths that a dialogue was going to be impossible. I became self-conscious that we were blocking her clientele from approaching. I nodded and stepped away with a stupid smile on my face. Tío Catarino reproached me as soon as we were out of earshot.

"You see, dummy? We each live in entirely different worlds, and yours is up there in the north. And that's where you'll stay."

I want to believe that had Abuela María been by my side, I would have been allowed to enter, been welcomed into their midst with an enthusiastic "¡Sési janongua je!" But I doubt it. I'll always be the foreigner from a country away.

I spent the last days of my trip strolling Avenida Francisco Madero, the main tourist stretch between the candy market and Las Tres Tarascas fountain. The great pink cathedral towered over all the other structures, which were mostly commercial buildings. During the day the traffic congested the historic district, but by evening the streets opened up, making way for pedestrians to wander about and poke fun at the tandem bikes with ten cyclist seats. The comical contraption was a popular tourist activity, but after a while one grew tired of hearing them chant nonsense as they pedaled in unison from one end of the avenue to the other.

I made repeated visits to the candy museum each time I remembered someone else I needed to bring back a gift to. And every other day I dropped in on the museum shop at el Templo de San Francisco at la Plaza Valladolid. The items were costly but exquisite. And since they claimed to put up more on display each day, I had to check in frequently.

At the entrance to the museum, independent vendors set up their stations. Since it was a month before Christmas, the merchandise favored artisan renditions of holiday decorations. Although I wasn't keen on the celebration, I bought a small wire Christmas tree with miniature Christmas balls that were tricolored to match the Mexican flag, and a nativity scene made with dry corn husk because it was gloriously colorful.

There were two Indigenous women sitting behind a long table displaying wool blankets and rebozos. I was drawn to them because they reminded me of Abuela María. I was also captivated by a queen-sized bedcover decorated with a deer pattern, a bird on each back, and a rebozo with monarch butterflies. The images were stitched on with colors that contrasted nicely with the white wool background.

"Is this your beautiful handiwork?" I asked.

"Of course," one of them answered.

"And where is home?"

"Zitácuaro," they said.

I recognized the name. It was the location of la Presa del Bosque, a dam that holds the water rumored to have curative powers. During Holy Week, people from all over Michoacán travel to find a miracle cure there. My aunts visited with my mother there on various occasions, hoping to improve her ailing health.

I suspected the women were not Purépecha but maybe Otomi or Mazahua, which was typical for that region. I didn't want to pry any further. But I wanted to document this encounter somehow. I asked them to pose with their work for a picture. They were reluctant, but I had paid them in cash without bargaining. They must have felt obligated. One of them even held the rebozo upside down. It wasn't until I looked at the pictures back in my rental that I recognized what an invasive and disrespectful thing I had done, basically pressuring the women to be photographed. Their faces looked uncomfortable, and this shamed me. How many times did I scoff at tourists doing the same? I resolved not to repeat this mistake again, and to apologize to them the next time I saw them.

The day before I was set to depart Michoacán, I had all but given up on the prospect of visiting the sanctuary. I decided to take advantage of the warmth and go out for an early morning stroll. The cathedral looked dazzling beneath the morning light. But just as I passed the kiosk, the same young lady who had delivered the bad news a few days earlier called out: "The butterflies have arrived! The butterflies have arrived!"

I became so flustered I couldn't even speak. But she knew what my intentions were when I pulled out my wallet. I was lucky enough to get the last seat on the tour bus, which was departing in minutes.

The drive to Angangueo was approximately five hours in that slow vehicle. But the views of the countryside were magnificent. These were the farmlands that were too exposed to be used for covert marijuana plantations. Here, the lands were for the livestock to graze, and every herd of cattle, goats, and sheep reminded me of a Michoacán that existed before the drug cartels invaded.

Once we reached the foot of the canyon, the guide informed us that we would have to climb part of the way by horse because the heavy rains had made the paths too slippery, and then the rest of the way—another hour's climb—on foot. Since the oyamel trees on this part of the mountain were hard for humans to reach, they were also less likely to be destroyed or damaged. After some initial grumbling by the other tourists, we forged ahead. The butterflies fluttering above us helped motivate our hike.

When I approached the horse, I was startled by its size. Suddenly the story Abuelo had told about falling off one of these animals became much more impressive. I grabbed the horn of the saddle with one hand, the grip of the cantle with the other, and with my feet badly adjusted to the stirrups, I started the steep climb. The horse trotted dangerously close to the edge of the trail, and I held my breath. The last thing I wanted was to go hurtling down the side of the mountain. But I made it to solid ground, which was lush green and blossoming with monarchs. It was Edenic.

Now came the more physically demanding part of the journey. I took heart when I saw a few older ladies ahead of me, but eventually they collapsed from exhaustion and had to be taken down on a stretcher, their purses dangling beneath them like extracted body organs. I then noticed many young men on the sides of the trail, waiting with stretchers beside them, and realized the climb was expected to defeat visitors like me. I was determined not to be one of them, but already I could feel the effects of the altitude. If I made it to the top, my stay would be cut short by the need to come down as quickly as possible. I had suffered from altitude sickness once before, in college while hiking with my school chums on the Sierra Nevada in California. The chill and dehydration felt familiar.

Somehow, I made it, with dozens of others, and now we were clustered together on a narrow part of the path. A rope prohibited people from going farther into the forest. The sky was overcast for the moment, which meant the butterflies would remain pressed to the trees for warmth. A guide told us that as soon as the sky cleared, the butterflies would cascade into the open. But we had to be very quiet. They were sensitive to noise.

More people arrived, and word was passed down, imploring silence. We became a community of quiet, like a congregation in a church during solemn prayer. The clouds began to disperse. Everyone kept still, even the children who had become impatient waiting for something to happen.

And then suddenly, something did. A waterfall of butterflies rained down from the tops of the trees, dispersing into the skies before they struck the ground. I couldn't help myself and I joined the communal gasp. That moment was the perfect blessing for a man like me who, like the butterflies, had also stayed away for far too long. But we finally made it. We had returned to find Michoacán changed, more hostile and melancholier than we had left it, but still home.

On my final night in Morelia, I walked about in la Plaza de los Mártires, right next to the cathedral. A group of Purépecha musicians was entertaining a crowd with folkloric music while four boys dressed as old men stomped on the ground, performing the traditional Danza de los Viejitos. Nearby a clown attracted a large gathering with his antics. His humor was a bit crass, yet this seemed to please the adults especially.

I might have sat there for the rest of the evening, but I decided I had some unfinished business at la Plaza Valladolid. The museum was closed for the day, but the vendors were still around, including the two women from Zitácuaro. This was my last chance to explain myself. I inched toward them as I browsed the other merchandise stands first.

My head was spinning. I wanted to let them know that my intention was not just to post their faces on social media as I bragged about my recent purchases. I wanted to remember them because they reminded me of Abuela María and I had few pictures of her, and none of her as the older woman I came to love. I could not see her anymore like Abuela Herminia and Abuelo Melecio because she was no longer alive. I had become estranged from my father's side of the family, the people who surely kept photographs of her. There was no one to ask for one, of Abuela María dancing or eating or drinking her can of beer in the afternoons as she waited for the tele-novelas to begin.

Abuela María was a memory in my head. I could not piece my loss together again the way I was gathering my beloved México around me back in New York City, one keepsake at a time.

But I didn't have the courage to speak to las señoras. When they saw me, they simply nodded. And I nodded back. What were we really but vendors and client? I was not their grandson or even distant relative. I was an American tourist, a descendant of Mexicans, who had come back to spend a few dollars on reminders of home. Tomorrow I would be gone, flown back to the safety and comforts of my privileges.

I said "Buenas noches" to them as I walked to the fountain in the center of the plaza. During the day, because of the heat, the plaza was mostly empty, and people sat on the side of the stone benches protected by shadow, either a tree's or that of the church. By sundown, the stone had cooled off and people squeezed into the benches, or the steps, or leaned against the fountain just as I was doing at that moment. The shoeshine stand had patient customers and the garbanzo seller set up his large tin on a low wooden stand, a saltshaker sticking out of his apron pocket. I breathed in the evening air, making a mental note about the wheat gorditas I had stored in the refrigerator of my Airbnb rental. Gorditas were a Purépecha delicacy. Of all the items I would take back with me, the sweetbread was my prized find even though that taste of Michoacán wouldn't last longer than a week or so. Still, it was worth it. Around me, children chased each other and screamed with gusto, each one of them taking for granted in their carefree joy that their loved ones were within reach.

FIRST INTERLUDE

The Wonder Woman T-Shirt

IT WAS MINE FIRST. I had picked it out from one of the large bins at the Goodwill thrift store, where my family went on weekends to buy second-hand clothes. I wouldn't step into a mall selling new clothing until my freshman year in college. As a fifteen-year-old kid, this was quite the find: a T-shirt in very good condition with one of my childhood idols—Wonder Woman. I didn't know her as Wonder Woman, however. I knew her as la mujer maravilla. Watching television in Michoacán meant that we were some-times a decade behind American TV shows and current on others. It was my great fortune to have powerhouse programming from the 1960s—*Hechizada* (*Bewitched*) and *Mi bella genio* (*I Dream of Jeannie*)—and the 1970s—*La mujer biónica* (*The Bionic Woman*) and *La mujer maravilla*—all at the same time.

I didn't think anything of the fact that all these shows had female leads. They were all blonde also, except for Wonder Woman, played by a brunette. Lynda Carter had Mexican ancestry. But I didn't find out about that until I was much older, which made her all the more meaningful. Having women at the center of the stories was not uncommon in Mexican TV, but this was mostly the case in telenovelas, where they suffered their way through a number of heartaches before finally getting married at the conclusion of the series. The realism of telenovelas and even comedy shows didn't appeal to me. At seven years old, I wanted fantasy. I wanted escape. And Samantha Stevens, Jaimie Sommers, Jeannie, and Diana Prince delivered.

The use of special effects in these American programs was mesmerizing, and nothing compared to their use in Mexican TV. But the real revelation came when I found out these shows were filmed in color. My maternal grandparents' small television with the awkward antenna had a black-and-white screen. My parents didn't own a television. Any chance I got, I would walk to my grandparents' house and watch my shows with my aunts, who were also fans. Abuela Herminia would sit in the corner doing her knitting and once in a while she would look up and declare that we should stop watching brujería—witchcraft. But it was spoken more out of a sense of duty than with conviction.

When one of my school friends, who lived across the street, invited me to her house to watch *La mujer biónica*, I was pleasantly surprised by how much more magical the show appeared on that large color TV. I had started to make a habit of going over to watch all four of my favorite shows until my younger brother, Alex, started tagging along. At one point, in one episode (I can't recall which show), a woman with a large belly appeared and my brother pointed and said, "That lady's pregnant."

Apparently, the neighbors were horrified. My friend's mother asked us to leave. I didn't know that we had been banned altogether until my mother forbid us to return. I protested and whined until she told me that the neighbor had been offended by something we had said and that it was best to keep our distance. "They're very religious," my mother added.

From that moment on, I went back to the black-and-white versions, but I was with my aunts, who were very expressive whenever Jeannie turned to smoke and got sucked back into her bottle, or whenever Samantha's mother, Endora, popped in and out of Samantha's living room. Watching with this audience was part of the fun. I had to imagine, however, that Jeannie's smoke was pink and that Endora's gown was green. From her big chair, Abuela Herminia mumbled, "Brujerías."

I knew not to beg my mother for a TV. Even as a boy I recognized that we were poor and that I shouldn't ask for much. And by the time my father came back from the north and bought us a color television, his pocket heavy with dollars, I had become less interested in the women and more interested in the men, like *El hombre nuclear* (*The Six Million Dollar Man*). I was also drawn to the handsome leading men in telenovelas, their names a mouthful like Víctor Alfonso or Francisco Xavier, their dress shirts opened too far down the middle of their chests, sometimes hairy, sometimes smooth and golden as honey.

At school, I was teased for my mannerisms. I smiled too much, I joined the girls in their circles, and I made faces at the boys. I didn't realize any of these habits about myself until they were pointed out, repeatedly. "You're going to grow up to be a woman if you don't stop lisping," one of the boys called out as I walked home with my book bag. I had to learn to walk forward without stopping to respond, even when the boys threw lumps of earth at my legs. Nearby, the men digging ditches simply laughed, which encouraged the boys to keep throwing.

Then, shortly after I turned ten, our family decided to relocate to California, my birthplace in a country I had no memory of. I didn't like the idea of getting torn away from Michoacán, but the prospect of starting over without the sissy reputation that had haunted me all these years became appealing. I could reinvent a better me.

For a brief period, however, before my mother and father could cross the border, Alex and I were sent to live with our father's parents, Abuelo Ramón and Abuela María.

From the moment we were picked up by Abuelo, I knew it was not going to be an easy situation. What began as excitement at the beginning of a new adventure quickly took a turn when I kept pointing at the livestock to ask Abuelo questions: "Are those cows for milk or for meat? Do they take those sheep up a mountain? Is there a mountain close by? Where are the shepherds? There isn't much grass around here. What do the animals eat?"

Exasperated, Abuelo barked at me without turning his head: "Stop asking stupid questions! And if you're going to ask questions, ask them like a man! You sound like a girl!"

Abuela didn't turn around. It was as if she hadn't heard anything at all.

I sunk back into my seat. That familiar taunt from my schoolmates back in Michoacán had crossed the border with me.

In an American school, it was easy to become invisible. I didn't speak the language, I couldn't communicate with most teachers, and there were so many kids that only the ones who misbehaved received any attention. I learned to keep my mouth shut and to keep all expression off my face, otherwise I would give myself away. But this tactic failed when I began to develop crushes on boys—boys who would respond, sometimes violently, if I tried to come near them.

"Get the fuck out of here, joto!" I would hear over and over again. But I couldn't resist this affinity I had for Mexican boys who spoke two languages and called themselves American; boys who made comments from the back of the classroom that everyone laughed at, sending the teacher into a tizzy; boys who demanded to be team captains and who scored the most points in soccer, basketball, baseball, and football; boys who were the center of the cafeteria ruckus and took liberties taking food from boys like me. I admired the power of their confidence. Wherever they stood, that's where they belonged. In the world of Americans and in the world of men, I felt out of place.

At home, I gravitated toward Abuela María. She wasn't affectionate but she was kind. Though at times she would have fun saying my nickname over and over again, Estuche de Oro, her coffer of gold, which she pronounced Estuchi, and then shortened to Tuchi. My brother was Beni, short for Beneficios, as in government benefits. These terms of endearment had to substitute for hugs or pecks on the cheek, which we didn't get.

Displays of affection were not practiced in Abuelo's household. Relatives who visited simply said "We're here!" when they arrived and "We're leaving!" as they left. The closest I ever got from Abuelo was a pat on the back when he was pleased that I had done something he approved of, which was seldom. More common were the scolding, the insults, and the reprimands about not doing things the more masculine way. Like cursing.

"You have to cuss like a man," he said after I yelled when I accidentally stubbed my toe. "Say 'Ay, cabrón' or 'Ay, güey,' not just 'Ay,' like a wimp."

I never liked cussing because my mother wouldn't permit it. Cussing was not allowed in Abuela Herminia's house either. And any other spectacles of vulgar behavior, like belching or crotch adjusting, were quickly met with disapproval. At Abuelo Ramón's table, a belch got a good laugh. So did farting and blaming Abuela María for it. And he had no qualms about adjusting himself as he walked out of the bathroom while the rest of us sat in the living room, watching TV. His antics were so common they became unnoticed. Except for his habit of not lifting the toilet seat when he went to the bathroom. That habit wasn't addressed until many years later, when my father came to visit.

"Apá," he said to Abuelo. "I'd like to ask you a huge favor to please lift the damn toilet seat!"

My brother and I were mortified yet relieved that this issue had finally been voiced.

Abuelo kept his gaze fixed on the TV as he said, "Tell your boys, too. They do it also."

I knew that Abuelo's disdain for my mannerisms was less about his homophobia and more about the fact that he looked at my brother and me as burdens. Alex gave Abuelo plenty to get angry about: failing grades, fighting in the playground, skipping school to hang out with our cousins, young men whom Abuelo never saw as anything besides troublemakers. But I was the well-behaved boy. He had to find something else to criticize and, like my school bullies, my feminine nature was an easy and convenient target.

Not long after our parents joined us, they moved in with Abuelo as well, and this only seemed to exacerbate his rage. There was never enough money. There was never enough food. There were too many mouths to feed. Our uncle had also moved in with his wife and three kids. And so did our aunt, with her brood of five. "And your boys eat like hogs," he would complain to my parents as he tossed spoons and slammed shut cupboard doors in the kitchen. "That Estuche, he's even beginning to look like a hog."

When I heard this, I blushed even though there was no one in the room with me. I sat hidden behind a book in the living room. When I read, no one bothered me. It was true that I had become a chubby kid. My baby fat had followed me into adolescence. Still, I got teased for being a sissy a lot more than for being overweight. Acting like a girl was the bigger offense.

The breaking point, however, was when my mother discovered Abuelo had become violently physical with me.

"What is that?" she asked when she discovered a bruise on my leg. "Who did that?"

"Abuelo," I said.

"Is this the first time he's done that?"

"No."

"Since when has he been doing that?"

I paused for a bit, trying to remember the first time Abuelo hit me. Yes, it was soon after Alex and I arrived. Abuelo had asked me to help bring in the groceries. The bags were heavy, but he handed them to me anyway. I wanted to show Abuelo that I was a strong boy, that I was a helpful boy, the boy who could follow directions. I was a good boy. But before I stepped inside, I tripped and the cans of tomato sauce came spilling out.

"Look at what you've done, useless! Pick them up before something gets lost."

I wasn't picking up the cans fast enough. It was getting dark, and I became anxious that I had failed the first test of my worth. Not to mention the first clear demonstration for Abuelo that, although I sounded like a girl, and acted like a girl, I was indeed, without a doubt, a boy.

Everything was back in the bags, or so I thought. I grabbed them tightly this time, unafraid of their weight. But as I walked inside the well-lighted living room, Abuelo called out to me.

"Here, you forgot one."

A can of tomato sauce came flying at me, and when it struck my head, I let go of the bags once again.

I couldn't tell my mother the whole story, but she wasn't asking for it. She only wanted an answer to her question, "Since when has he been doing that?"

"Since I arrived," I said to her.

Not long after, my father moved our family of four out of Abuelo's house. And so too my uncle fled with his family, and my aunt with hers. Abuelo and Abuela moved to a smaller house across from the post office, and then later qualified for subsidized housing at El Campo, two towns away. Not long after that, my mother died, and back we were with Abuelo, only three of us this time. My father promised us that things were going to change, and they did somewhat. Abuelo never laid a hand on me again, and I was determined not to give him an excuse either. I withdrew into a dark corner of the room, unheard and barely seen in my sadness. The only saving grace was that I had to enroll in a different school. It was a fresh start. A chance to reinvent myself all over again. This time I was determined to succeed.

Though Abuelo kept his promise to my father, I was careful not to slip. The best way was to simply not speak. Abuela commented on this to Abuelo as they sat down to eat roasted peanuts. I was in my corner, reading a library book. "Look at Tuchi over there," she said. "He doesn't make a sound at all."

"As it should be," Abuelo said. There was no malice in his voice. It was more like a statement of victory. After all these years, I had been tamed.

The only time I ventured outside was when Abuelo dropped Abuela and me at the Goodwill thrift store. We spent hours rummaging through the bins of clothing, moving items on the crowded display shelves, and poking fun at the eccentric older ladies who walked in to try out hats from another era and coats that looked like fur but felt thorny like a cactus. I went back and forth between joining Abuela to make comments about the other shoppers and browsing the bookcases packed with mass paperbacks at the back of the store.

During one of these visits, I discovered the Wonder Woman T-shirt. Suddenly, I was reminded of my days in Michoacán, sitting with my mother's sisters, who giggled and cheered whenever Diana Prince spun and spun until her bun came loose and after the flash of lightning, when Wonder Woman stood in her skin-tight superhero outfit. A few seconds later she was bending steel rods or tossing oversized crates or lifting cars or leaping from the ground to the top of a building. Invincible and unstoppable, she had arrived to save the world, to save us all.

But what really convinced me that this was the version of Wonder Woman that I needed was her picture: slightly turned to the side, ready for battle with her magic lasso looped around her hip, smoke in the background suggesting that she had just completed her transformation from prim and proper intelligence officer to Amazon warrior. There she was, my childhood idol, in black and white, exactly as I had learned to appreciate her on that black-and-white TV.

"Can I get this, Abuela?"

Abuela lifted the bottom of the white T-shirt to inspect the image closely. "Who is this woman?" she asked.

"La mujer maravilla," I responded.

"La mujer maravilla?" Abuela looked at it with disinterest for a few more seconds before saying, "Put it in the cart."

I wasn't intending to ever wear the T-shirt. It was more like a memento, a photograph, a small reminder of the happiness I once felt long before I was moved from one country to another, torn away from my mother's family to live with my father's. I must have stored it in a safe place to keep it a secret, so well hidden that I completely forgot about it when, a few years later, I moved out of the house for good to enroll at the university. I had made up my mind to move out of my grandparents' as soon as I could because, of all the things that made me vulnerable—poverty, violence, family secrets—being gay was what could get me killed. I was certain of that.

College was yet another new beginning, though this time I was not going to be what the bullies wanted me to be—I was going to be myself. And for thirty years I managed it. Mine wasn't a smooth journey but it was mine exclusively, bad decisions, good decisions, failures and triumphs. I didn't receive much news from home except when somebody passed away. Like Abuelo. And then Abuela.

Then one evening, scouring Facebook out of curiosity to see pictures of the relatives I had left behind decades ago, I came across a photograph of Abuelo and Abuela posing with Tío Ramón and his two daughters, the oldest almost as tall as Abuelo. Abuela wore one of her aprons, this one pink, but Abuelo stood proudly in my Wonder Woman T-shirt. Except that he had cut off the sleeves to expose his shoulders and thin biceps. He did this to all his T-shirts because he believed it made him look manlier.

I had expected to feel outrage at the defilement of what was once an important connection to a better period of my life. But seeing him looking frail and harmless after all these years awoke a soft spot that I didn't know

I had inside. It was a kind of tenderness tinged with sympathy and perhaps nostalgia that I'm certain all middle-aged men develop for their adolescence, when everything seemed terrible but with the passage of time now didn't seem as painful as all that. Or maybe that was what coming to terms with the past did to a person. It was closure, letting the wounds heal and arriving at this miraculous new place called forgiveness.

Ancestry

Here you say one. Over there they say uno. We say ma.

—Abuela's lessons in Purépecha

MY FATHER'S PROCLAMATION that Abuela was full-blooded Purépecha was his way of clinging to his ancestry. He himself was not full-blooded because Abuelo was a descendant of mestizos, that mix of Indigenous and Spanish blood that dated back to Hernán Cortés and his translator and courtesan Malinche. (The conversation has shifted in recent years because not all Mexicans have Spanish or Indigenous blood. But my family line is mestizo through and through.) After my father married my mother, who didn't claim any Indigenous ancestry, I knew I was even less Purépecha than my father.

My skin color was not as dark as Abuela's or my father's, both of whom were as dark as the Purépechas I came across in Michoacán. I was simply mestizo brown, with features that leaned toward my European blood or toward my Indigenous—it all depended on who was making the determination. In México, I was Mexican. In New York City, I was Puerto Rican, except to Nuyoricans, who usually assumed I was Colombian. I didn't resemble the Indigenous Poblanos of the area, who were the most recognizable Mexicans.

I didn't obsess with identity, nor did I do much to correct anyone's mislabeling of my ethnicity. I actually liked being identity fluid. When I traveled to Puerto Rico, I picked up their Caribbean accent, and very few people questioned my mimicry. In Spain, I was Mexican, not American, especially if I revealed my name, Rigoberto—a Spaniard name that had flourished like many others in the Americas long after the colonial period. Getting pegged as Mexican right away didn't bother me. Besides, I felt safer as a Mexican than as an American in Europe, given how unpopular Americans were now and again.

In México, I was considered a moneyed Mexican because I spent generously on arts and crafts and sought out the best restaurants in the places I visited. But I was different, or so I was told by waiters, shop owners, and shoeshine boys, which was just a polite way of saying they knew I was gay, but acceptably gay, as in not too feminine. This toning down of my mannerisms was another form of self-preservation. Yet this didn't stop some shop employees from having fun.

"Look at these, señor. Perfect for your wife, ¿no?" a middle-aged woman said to me, showing me a pair of earrings.

I turned from the wall of pottery, which is what drew me into the shop in the first place. I had become interested recently with the clayware of Capula and Tlaquepaque. Her smile was pleasant, so I wanted to decline gently.

"No thank you," I said. "I'm not married."

"Not married?" The woman feigned shock. "How can that be? Well, there's time, you're still young."

During checkout, the woman took one last shot: "I was just saying to myself, how can that attractive man not have a wife? And with such excellent taste!"

I smiled and averted my eyes, affirming yet again that in México it was not my ambiguous ethnicity that drew much attention but my sexuality. I placed my purchases in a sturdy tote bag I carried over my shoulder, remembering that time a boy squatting next to his mother at the flea market pointed to me and sing-songed, "He's-got a-baaag, he's-a-laaady, he's-a-laaady."

His mother quickly swatted him upside the head. "Men can also carry bags nowadays. Be quiet!"

I laughed it off and kept going. The sting of embarrassment was small, but still a sting.

No one ever mentioned other gay men in the family, though I knew they existed. Once my gaydar was fully developed, I could pick them out in the family gatherings. But nothing was said between us. If anything, we kept away from each other as much as we could after initial introductions.

Since I didn't have much contact with my Purépecha relatives, I didn't know much about their views on homosexuality. In Oaxaca among the Zapotec people, the Muxes were considered a third gender and usually accepted into a society that did not believe in disowning a person who could contribute to Zapotec life. But they were not called gay—that was nomenclature from the outside. With the Purépecha, Catholicism had taken a firm hold on the culture. Abuela María was quite a believer herself, though we rarely went to church. I always thought this was one of Abuelo's whims, but much later I realized that for Abuela, her Catholicism was personal. She rarely preached about it, though once in a while I caught a glimpse of her devoutness.

One afternoon after the high school bus dropped us off, Abuela stopped Alex and me to point to a piece of paper she had framed awkwardly and hung on the wall, above the television. Pictured prominently was Pope John Paul II waving his hand in blessing. His image appeared lifted from a photograph as he rode his popemobile past an adoring crowd.

"With that document, we don't need to pray anymore," Abuela explained. "That document says that each time the pope prays, he's praying for all of us in this family."

As she said this, I detected the sentimentality in her eyes—a watery look that made me want to embrace her, but I held back because we didn't do hugs. My brother and I looked at each other, unsure of how to respond. We simply nodded. What bothered me was that our family name on that certificate was handwritten in scribbly blue ink and without capitalization. I didn't ask Abuela where she bought it. I knew, even though she didn't say, that this was a local purchase and likely a money-making scheme. But Abuela believed in it so I didn't question it. For her it was a genuine connection to God.

I had a complicated relationship to God. I had turned to religion for solace after the death of my mother when I was twelve years old. My brother and I fulfilled one of my mother's wishes that we comply with the holy sacrament of First Communion. I held on to the prayers and lessons, reciting them each night until I began to feel those unwelcomed urges during puberty.

The more I fantasized about boys and men, the more I detached myself from my religious teachings. They seemed incompatible with my eroticized imagination. I knew that what I was feeling, what I was becoming, was not going to change, so I simply let go of what made me feel shame. This was my secret, however. And I never revealed my sexuality to anyone until college. I didn't come out publicly until graduate school.

The only hint I had of Abuela's opinion of gay people came by way of a daytime talk show on Spanish-language television. I walked across the living room, between the TV and my grandparents, to get to the kitchen for a drink of water. Abuelo seemed particularly amused by the discussion on that stage set with two women sitting side by side and holding hands. The interviewer was polite and inquisitive, the women responded with calm, but the audience was breathless, stunned into silence. Those two women were lovers. Lesbians.

I stood at a distance as I drank my water. Each time the women spoke about their private home life—nothing too out of the ordinary or particularly scandalous—Abuelo would burst out laughing. By contrast, Abuela flicked her hand at the screen as an act of rejection, voicing her disgust with an odd *Nah!* sound.

Other than that episode with the talk show, there was never any discussion about homosexuality in my presence. I knew there had to be homosexual Purépechas, but since that side of the family had such a different language and culture, I didn't expect to find out if there was a different reception to them outside the intolerance and derision that had been instilled on the Indigenous population by Catholicism. When I traveled to México, I told the shop workers and waiters and shoeshine boys that I was Purépecha, as a way to amplify my Indigenous pride and hopefully overshadow my sexual identity. It certainly gave the chit-chat a focus away from my marital status. With my family, however, the distancing was much more severe.

I disappeared as soon as I left for college at seventeen. I had a way out via an education. And I would come to understand that many of us queer boys fled to the universities as a way to earn respectability but also to keep us away from the inquisitive tías. Being at a university meant that we had a higher purpose and were too busy to pursue women or even consider marriage. Career came first. Little did our tías know that on weekends we squeezed into tight shirts before gathering at the gay clubs to drink Long Island iced teas, dance until closing, and hopefully make out with a willing stranger who was also in line to use the bathroom. We nursed the hangover on Sunday, aggressively. By Monday we were back at the desk, drinking coffee and diet sodas to keep us alert as we double-checked the formatting on an essay.

I reappeared in the Coachella Valley periodically during the next two decades, over Thanksgiving or during the summers, just after the grape harvest was over in the Coachella Valley. Each time, Abuela would comment on how much thinner I was getting. My cousins remarked on how much fatter I looked. And older. That my hairline was running away from my forehead. Everyone stopped asking about girlfriends or marriage by the time I turned thirty-three. They inquired about my teaching job and had nothing to say about my writing except that they thought it was a pity that I was like a traveling salesman with a suitcase full of books and a tired sales pitch. Have I tried selling my books at the flea markets? My cousin Mari said her brother-in-law, El Chofe, sold burned music CDs. Maybe we should team up one day.

After the initial greetings, everyone settled into their usual routines and I sat in the corner of the room, interesting only to the children who were curious about this stranger who had walked into their houses as if he belonged there, who would disappear in a few days and not be seen again until many months later when they had to be reminded that they had met me before. Abuelo offered to cut my hair like he used to when I was still living at home. Tía Melania made plans to cook chiles rellenos because I told her years ago that no Mexican restaurant came close to her savory method—soaked in stew and stuffed with picadillo, a dish I could never find on any menu. I couldn't shake the feeling that I remained frozen in an earlier, more innocent version. They knew how to interact with that person who was certainly a virgin, most likely asexual, and dedicated fully to his schooling. My only companions in bed had to be a laptop and books. Without admitting to a partner or a dating life, I had no personal history. Unbeknownst to them, I had experienced one breakup after another; had sweated it out, waiting for the results of an HIV test; and had made a promise yet again to make sure to use condoms. But within the year I would be back at the STD testing site. When I decided to stop visiting everyone except my brother, the only person I had informed that I was gay, no one came searching or picked up the phone. That young man from long ago was inconsequential to their daily lives anyway and was relegated to memory and a few anecdotes from the past, when he was still a boy. I knew this for a fact because that's how they talked about the dead.

In truth, I didn't miss them either, except for the home-cooked meals. Those children who stared at me apprehensively during my rare sightings at home became adolescents and then husbands and wives, and then parents. If I saw them again, I wouldn't recognize any of them. But it's more likely that I'll never see them. If they have inherited the stories from the generation before them, I might make a cameo or serve as a side note, a minor player in the timeline of their family histories. The people who knew me the longest were growing old and forgetful. They will eventually die. Soon I will vanish altogether, my name turned to a dust that doesn't stir with the storytelling breath.

By leaving for good, I made a deliberate choice to remove myself from the family pictures so that they never had to engage in the uncomfortable conversations about my private life. In my Mexican household, homosexuality was an ingredient in vulgar jokes and insults. In México it was even worse. My family in Michoacán was extremely religious and warned me not to stay out too late because the predatory homosexuals were about. The times I stayed in town past sundown, I looked and looked and never found them. The only homosexual about was me.

My vanishing didn't keep me up at night. I had lived a full life out of earshot of my family. I became financially independent, flourished in my career, and have had a string of hookups, lovers, and significant others. I was relatively unbothered until I arrived at the startling realization that this choice to distance myself may not have been as unusual as I had always believed. Worse yet, I realized that I may have learned this method of self-preservation from the other homosexuals in my family.

—

Mamá Lola was from the small town of Nahuatzen, where Abuela and her siblings were also born and raised. The Carrillo Maldonado family grew exponentially with each generation, but the storytelling always included the humorous anecdotes of years past, tales too entertaining to be forgotten. That's how we knew about family members that many of us had never really met, like Tío Demetrio, who slept on a chair, and Tía Renata, who was called Tía Piñata because of the way her body and skirt swayed and swung when she walked. Others were barely mentioned, like Mamá Lola's brother, or perhaps it was her cousin. I heard about him quite accidentally, while I was half-listening to the grown-ups in conversation.

"Who knows whatever happened to him," one adult said.

"Spain is so far away," said another, which was another way of saying they didn't expect him to return. The pregnant pause that followed was a gesture of resignation.

That moment stayed with me. I knew of no one else who had traveled that far. Whenever I could, I asked questions until I pieced together the narrative: he had been working for a Spanish family in México, until the Mexican Revolution forced them back to their country. They took with him their trusty servant, a handsome Purépecha with pretty eyes, who went willingly in search of adventure. It was fine; he wasn't married.

I say "he" because I have forgotten his name. And all those people who remembered him are gone. But after my own vanishing, I began to reconsider that story: the way family members mentioned his pretty eyes, the way they added the detail of his bachelorhood. Were these euphemisms, polite ways of signaling that he was definitely not like the rest of the men, that his uniqueness was not confined to his separation from his loved ones and country?

When I finally traveled to Spain myself, I looked for him in the crowd. It was a useless endeavor because he had likely passed away decades before. Still, I wanted to experience something, like the sensation that I was walking on the same paths that my Indigenous ancestor had, and that he had loved his life despite the homesickness. I wanted to believe that he was happy and free to be himself. I wanted him not to have regretted his decision because at the time I had already done the same: disappeared.

As the awareness of my own difference became palpable, I latched on to the story of an uncle who had the unbecoming nickname Gallina. His name was Ignacio, but Mamá Lola called him Igna, which eventually became Ina, which changed completely to Gallina. I never met Gallina because he too had disappeared, though in this case everyone knew where he was: living on the coast of Michoacán. He slept on the beach. He had no home. He drew sketches of the beachgoers for coins. Someone had bumped into him once, and they reported back that those sketches were inappropriate. To my conservative family, this might have meant that he captured the sensuality of people in bathing suits. Drawing women was offensive enough, but men too? Despite this self-imposed poverty, he had achieved autonomy. Oh, yes, and he had never married.

And then there was that cousin who I never met but had seen on various occasions in Tía Juana's living room. There he was pictured in the faraway land of Canada. He was likely the first one in the family who had walked on snow, she bragged. In another photograph, he was riding a horse. Nothing new around these parts of Michoacán, but this was a Canadian horse. They were much larger, Tía Juana stated with authority. "Isn't he handsome?" she asked, though she likely didn't expect me to answer. So I didn't. I stared at the photograph, unsettled by the warmth that suddenly coursed through my body. "Unfortunately, he will never marry," Tía Juana said. He was too busy, apparently, seeking adventure with his companion. When she showed me a picture of the two men with their arms around each other, I sensed that their closeness was much more than friendship.

These three men gave me some kind of orientation, even when I suspected that perhaps I was projecting. I had no way of confirming if indeed they were gay, but I was in the same situation as they were. I was the one who had strayed from home, who was the eccentric artist, who was deemed too distracted by my travels to have time to consider settling down.

I also saw the alternative narrative in my family. There were three others whom I recognized as gay, but all three were locked in the closet in order to remain at home. Two of them did marry. The third couldn't because he was too preoccupied taking care of his aging parents.

Given a choice between disappearing at home or disappearing to claim my freedom, I chose the latter. But like my father, I wanted to cling to something bigger than my individual story, something that reclaimed me, something that was unquestionable and inextricable from my being: Abuela's Purépecha bloodline.

—

By 2017, the ancestry craze was still hot. There were a number of services that offered to study one's DNA and determine percentages of ethnic origins. Henry Louis Gates Jr.'s *Finding Your Roots* was in its fifth season, with no signs of waning in popularity. Time and again, friends of mine who were Mexican came back to brag about their results. In most cases, the percentage of Indigenous blood was just under or just over 40 percent.

"I know I'm way more than that," I boasted, and then echoed my father's phrase, "My grandmother was a full-blooded Purépecha."

Still, I wasn't convinced to send for a testing kit. Besides, there was already griping about how this DNA information was being co-opted by pharmaceutical companies, or how it could eventually be seized by the federal government to trace the family lineages of felons or alleged terrorists. All these wild conspiracy theories only made me want to wait until there was irrefutable proof that this expensive venture was legitimate.

That evidence came by way of a casual conversation with my friend Sergio in New York. We were meeting for lunch when out of the blue he began to chuckle.

"What's so funny?" I asked.

"I can't stop thinking about my stupid brother." He moved the fork around in his cup of coleslaw. We met at Artie's, a popular deli in Upper West Side Manhattan, which was close to his apartment. "You have to try their famous roast beef sandwich," he had told me in order to convince me to travel all the way from my apartment in Queens to his neighborhood yet again. I knew it was mostly a ploy to get me to make the inconvenient trek, but I didn't mind because I rarely came to this part of town and it was a chance to try eateries that I didn't frequent as a regular. I didn't know this then, but soon after our lunch date, Artie's would shut its doors after eighteen years in business.

"What happened?" I prompted.

"You know about that DNA ancestry thing?" I nodded my head. "Well, my brother took it and he found out that he had a match somewhere in the country. He called me to tell me that he suspected our father might have had a love child, and that maybe we should contact this mystery sibling through the DNA testing service." Sergio cackled.

"What's funny about that?"

"What's funny," Sergio said, "is that the match is me! I took the same DNA test without telling him. And I didn't know that he had taken it. But if it was me who had received that notification first, I would have assumed my brother had taken it too, not jump to ridiculous conclusions."

"So, it *does* work," I said.

"DNA testing? Yes, it's scientific."

Inspired by Sergio's anecdote, I sent for the testing kit.

When it finally arrived, I spat into the test tube, mailed it back to the labs, and forgot about it until the results came back via email.

As I suspected, my Indigenous percentage was notable, 70 percent, though the grid called it Native American. I was 16 percent Iberian peninsular ancestry—the Spanish blood in me. And then there was a surprising percentage of Portuguese (4 percent) and Southern Italian (3 percent), but I had no interest or curiosity about either. I called all those friends who had flaunted their 40–45 percent Indigenous ancestry.

"I told you," I repeated in each conversation. "My grandmother was a full-blooded Purépecha."

That brief period of excitement and sharing the results with my brother led to a nostalgic conversation about Abuela.

"Remember when she was trying to teach us words in Purépecha?" I asked.

"Yeah. Do you remember any?"

"Ichúskuta," I said.

"Everyone knows that one," my brother said, unimpressed. He then added, "Remember that time she was teaching us to count?"

The memory suddenly sparked into consciousness. I had forgotten about that moment altogether.

"We say ma," she said, holding out one finger. "Uno. And here they say one."

I wasn't sure if my brother had been as interested as I was. My brother and I were Spanish speakers when we migrated to the U.S. We had to adopt English the way she had to adopt Spanish.

She showed us the rest of the numbers using her fingers: tsimani (2), tanímu (3), t'amu (4), iúmu (5), kuímu (6), iúmu tsimani (7), iúmu tanímu (8), iúmu t'amu (9), témbeni (10).

The more numbers she named, the farther I felt from her. And the DNA results didn't bring me any closer.

I didn't give the DNA testing service much thought after that, though I was repeatedly invited to subscribe to their other services, like contacting potential relatives. But with such a large and complicated family that I had parted ways with some time ago, I wasn't eager to reconnect with new ones. Not on the American side of the border anyway.

Two years later, however, one of them contacted me.

A notification alerted me to the fact that someone was trying to reach me. I didn't have to subscribe to the service to read the message. I expected it was one of my cousins, who had also taken the test. Like Sergio, I kept my cool and had no expectations about anything. But then I opened the email dated August 27, 2019, from a woman named Alaina:

"Hello! I'm looking to find a photo of my father and you're one of the only DNA matches on my biological father's side. If you have any information on [REDACTED] 11/19/1971 please message me back!"

On January 16, 2020, I received a follow-up message:

"He was born in Mexico but lived in Hemet California in late 80s–early 90s. I don't have much information unfortunately."

Alaina's middle and last names were not Mexican. I assumed that this was her married name or her adopted family's name or her mother's maiden name. Regardless, she was a love child alright. My family had produced many. Abuelo had. So had my father. These children were mostly estranged from the family, their existences hushed or never acknowledged. If they eventually stepped out of the shadows, they were adults by then, and the furor or scandal had sputtered out long ago. Now they were simply vestiges of a past, reminders of some youthful indiscretion that had come to shake hands with the middle-aged men who had never claimed them. Their return was met with little excitement, like finding an old sweater that had been deemed lost and then recovered by the time the owner could no longer wear it again because they had outgrown it. But the small spark of recognition was still there.

"You're so big," the men would say, because they had leapt over their children's entire childhood and adolescence. And they would never ask about the mother. Not while their current wives were still alive. That would have been a step too far.

And then these love children would vanish as quietly as they had appeared because they did not come looking for a father but for the man who had contributed half of his DNA. *So, that's where I get my nose! So, that's why I'm curly haired!* The entire exchange would remain at the surface because nothing more would be offered and nothing more would be asked for. There was no time to compare temperaments or habits, those characteristics that people learned to identify with prolonged contact. What you saw at first glance was what you got, like looking at a photograph, distant and two-dimensional.

And a photograph is all Alaina wanted. Not a phone number or even news of her father's fate. At forty-nine, surely, he was still alive, though no longer living in California or even in the U.S. Her messages intrigued me, which is why I didn't answer right away. I spent time studying her words to try to figure out how I was going to respond, if ever.

She was not looking for a father-daughter reunion. Perhaps she thought or was told that her father was dead. The scarcity of information told me that she had been kept apart from any telling details, except the few that she noted, which probably came from her own birth certificate. She was most likely under thirty, maybe as young as twenty. Certainly somewhere in between. The message did not reveal where she was writing from, but those exclamation marks betrayed a thrill that she had stumbled upon a pathway to an answer she had long been seeking.

It might have been easier to simply message back and tell her, "No, I don't know where your father is. In fact, I don't even know him, even though we're close cousins." But that would have been a lie.

"What do you think?" I asked one of my graduate students named Zeus while we were taking a walk through the park during the COVID-19 pandemic. I was now living in Newark, New Jersey. The shutdown had lifted, though I remained quarantined, anxious about becoming infected. Since he lived nearby, we felt safe enough to take weekly strolls to Branch Brook Park on early Friday mornings. Masks required.

"Why shouldn't she know the truth? It's her father. It's her decision to make if she wants to contact him or find out more about him."

"It's just that . . ." I hesitated. Suddenly I found myself in a strange predicament. There were other subjects besides homosexuality that were not supposed to be said out loud, and certainly not shared with people outside the family circle.

Zeus and I crossed paths with other walkers, a few joggers, and even a small group of Black women doing yoga, their colorful mats splayed over the sidewalk and spilling into the road. Very few people were not wearing face masks, which is why I kept coming back week after week. This exercise was a remarkable contrast to my day during the shutdown, which would have driven me stir crazy had I not had a small balcony I could step into and breathe some fresh air.

"You know, I know about her father. He's not a good person. Or rather, he did something horrible."

My student's eyes softened.

"He's in a Mexican prison. That's why she hasn't been able to Google him. Records in Mexico are not as public as they are in the U.S."

We reached the end of our path in the park. On the small hill, towering over Newark's North Ward, was the Basilica of the Sacred Heart, the fifth-largest cathedral in the country. Its French Gothic Revival style gave it an indulgent splendor that seemed out of place in the working-class part of town. But that's what churches and other religious buildings were supposed to do: demonstrate greatness and maintain a highly visible presence so that its purpose was not easily ignored or forgotten.

"It's going to break her heart," I said as I sat on a stone bench with a view of the cathedral.

"But you're not responsible for that," Zeus said. "He is."

"I'll think about it," I said. "I already waited seven months to respond. What's a few more days?"

I spent the rest of the weekend staring at Alaina's name for inspiration, as if at any moment it could animate and plead with me to make a decision. Imagining myself in her situation didn't help. I let people go easily, from lovers to friends to relatives. With relatives it was complicated but directly connected to Alaina's father, or rather his actions. My cousin was a sex offender, imprisoned for crimes committed against children. I found it ironic how homosexuals were not as protected as child molesters. Not in our family tree, which had shaken the branches through the generations and cut the gay men loose. But the pedophiles got to hide among the leaves.

When I finally made up my mind to message Alaina back, I decided to be direct and clear: "Good afternoon, cousin. Forgive the late reply but I had to think carefully before I responded. I don't have access to a picture of your father because I'm cut off from the family. I can send you a few names to make further inquiries through Facebook. All I know is that your father is incarcerated. It's a rather sensitive situation and I wanted to prepare you for that in case you were going to pursue this further. Let me know what I can do to help."

As soon as I pressed send, I regretted mentioning that he was incarcerated. But I knew my family. I knew they would ignore her entirely in order to keep from voicing the unthinkable. On their Facebook pages, there was zero mention of my cousin's fate or existence. He had been disappeared because he had been caught. The pedophiles who had not been caught had Facebook pages plastered with pictures of their ordinary but public lives. But the stories were starting to come to light.

I didn't hear back from Alaina again. Whether she pursued her goal despite the revelation or if she simply deleted my message and regretted writing to me in the first place, I'll likely never find out. But I do know about standing at the crossroads before making a decision. Both directions have consequences. It's not a question of which path leads to less suffering but rather which path leads to pain that one can endure for a lifetime.

When I spoke to my brother about it, he simply said, "It's sad."

Yes, it was sad. Sad that we had become the pariahs from my cousin's born-again Christian family, Alex because he had been living in sin with a woman he hadn't married and me because I was gay. They harbored a pedophile. And as soon as he was finally released, we suspected that they might take him back. Child molestation was forgivable, apparently.

We found out later that they were also hardcore Republicans. Trump supporters. Which was another irony.

"Remember how mean they were to us because we had been born in the U.S. and any chance they got they called us gringos?" my brother said.

"And now we're probably not patriotic enough," I said.

Perhaps that's why I was hungering for community outside the border crossers. I respected my family's struggles to adapt to the U.S. and find jobs that would take us out of poverty. But that didn't mean we were immune to the hideous human flaws. I wanted to see past the immediate history, and those childhood memories that continued to keep me up at night. I wanted to enter Abuela's world—get lost in it—because it was intriguing and mysterious, but in lovely ways. I wanted to claim Purépecha ancestry, because the Mexican one had disappointed me too many times.

Uandakuntani is the closest translation to the word "secret" in Purépecha. It means to accuse someone, to reveal someone's hidden behavior. Alaina, if she kept seeking, would find out what my cousin's family was trying to keep quiet, what I also knew, and had kept silent about all this time.

Mañosos

Here you say two. And over there they say dos. We say tsimani.

—Abuela's lessons in Purépecha

AFTER MY MOTHER DIED WHEN I WAS TWELVE, I descended into depression. Without my mother, there was one less adult I could hide behind. Her absence cleared a wider path to my body. I began losing weight. White splotches invaded my anemic face. I missed numerous days of school, wrapping myself like a mummy at home as I slept most of the day, recovering rest I had lost staying awake at night.

"You hardly speak up," my teachers said to me tenderly when I returned. They had been told that my mother had died. That must explain it. They let me sit in the back of the room, inaudible and, most of the time, invisible.

One morning, as I sat at the dining table, staring at the egg and beans Abuela María had served me, I informed her that I didn't feel well enough to go to school.

"Again?" she said. "Your grandfather's going to get angry."

This was her way of warning me that I had two choices: go to school and spend a few hours in the nurse's office or stay home and listen to Abuelo gripe about having to look after me. She was going to work at the packinghouse. Her ride was on its way.

"There's something going on," Abuela said.

I lowered my head.

"Why don't you tell me, Tuchi," she said. "What's wrong?"

She was a gentle woman, but I didn't expect her to comfort me with a touch or a caress. No one in our family did that. When I felt too weak to

56

last the entire school day, Abuelo would have to come pick me up. In front of the school officials, he was soft-spoken and even tried to greet me with a hug that was so awkward it felt like he was simply resting his elbows on my shoulders. But once in the truck he scolded me and complained about the waste of gas. That was the extent of his interactions with me during that time. Abuela was at work all day, and after work she was too tired to do anything more than drink a beer and watch TV. That morning's invitation to confide in her was unusual.

"Is somebody doing something to you? Maybe at school?"

I shook my head. Hot tears started to well in my eyes. But even that stopped when she asked unexpectedly, "Is somebody in the family doing something to you?"

A rush of goosebumps pimpled my entire body. Even though I had no intention of speaking, I felt my throat lock. Yet I was unsure about how to read that question. Did she mean getting bullied or harassed by my brother or Tío Ramón? Or did she mean something more serious? I remained silent because I didn't want to risk misunderstanding her.

"Because there are nasty people out there," she said. She used the word "mañoso," which we used innocently with children who were being mischievous. But applied to grown-ups there was a whole other level of suggestion, as in perversion.

I didn't dare look at Abuela, afraid that my look would give me away. Besides, I was mortified that my behavior had pushed her into this line of thinking. I didn't want her near this darkness. She belonged in the light, laughing at the silliest things, like when Abuelo walked out of the shower with a piece of soap stuck to his hair. Or when he farted in his room, loud enough for all the household to hear. Sometimes on the weekends she played pirekuas at full volume. Or rather Abuelo did, as a way to compete with the neighbors across the street who played Los Bukis, a Mexican band whose music he detested. Abuela walked around the apartment. She was so delighted to hear music from her homeland and in her language that she bounced a few steps in the living room. And if the cat happened to pass by, she grabbed it as her dance partner.

"You're not going to tell me?" Abuela pressed on.

I heard her far away. My body kept floating back until the car beeped outside, which shook us both back to the mundane. Abuela put her pointing finger to her lips, affirming that this exchange was to be kept a secret. She picked up her work bag with her coffee thermos and lunch, said goodbye, and walked out the door. I remained fixed to the chair, staring at the eggs that had grown cold and unappealing.

Abuela didn't pick up on that conversation after work or any other time, though sometimes I caught her staring at me from across the room, deep in thought. We locked eyes for a few seconds until one of us became uncomfortable and broke the spell by turning away.

What haunted me over the years was that finger to the lips, a command to hush. She had made that gesture before, but for more innocent reasons, like when she slipped me spending money or I broke a dish and she quietly scooped it up. There was only one person we were keeping this from, and that was Abuelo. Whether he would actually be displeased that Abuela was being generous with me or annoyed that I had caused an accident in the kitchen, I wasn't sure, but we were taking precautions anyway. That was the secret of Abuelo's control: we didn't know how he would react, but the threat of his reaction was enough to keep us in line.

But the hush finger of that fateful morning was different. And since we never discussed it again, it turned out to be definitive. I didn't blame Abuela. Keeping quiet was one way to survive in this family because we were stuck with each other. What was the point of bringing to light things that would shame us even more? When the adults felt particularly aggrieved, they would threaten to leave. And if they left, they eventually returned. The initial offense would be one more grudge to hold against someone. The next argument would be heavy with bad blood. Our family rarely had conflict with anyone outside the inner circle because there was plenty to deal with at home.

When I first revealed to a close friend that I had been molested as a child, he said, "Thank you for sharing that with me. I'm glad I can help you carry the weight of that burden from now on." Indeed, I did feel something lifting, as if my head had been opened like a jar and something restless had been set free.

When I was a teenager experiencing puberty, I blamed my sexuality on the molestation. Surely being touched by a man had caused this. And it wasn't only one man.

As a boy I had experimented with neighbors and school friends who were my age. Those interactions, which we knew were forbidden, were curiosity mixed with the thrill of transgression—that getting away with something that made us feel less like boys and more like grown-ups, even if it was simply looking at each other's private parts. Fitting a baby penis between the ticklish ass cheeks was an act accompanied by giggles. But there was complicity, otherwise this clandestine playtime could not remain secret. And if it spilled into the streets, we risked getting punished by our parents, reprimanded by our priest, and ostracized by the other boys.

Those adult male hands crawling under the sheets, caressing me in the dark while I was falling asleep, or worse, while I was heavily asleep and awakened by the prodding of fingers, was not a welcomed feeling. No permission had been sought and none granted, but there I was, suddenly paralyzed as if pretending to be dead would repel those hands. I didn't have to see the person to know who it was because I had caught him looking at me strangely earlier in the day. It was a look I recognized whenever I saw it, a piercing look that caged me from afar. I was being marked. When I finally understood that I had been caught, it was too late to escape, or scream, or fight back. And I reentered that space between shadow and light, between being oblivious and well aware of what was being taken from me. That's what it felt like. These men came to collect another piece of me each time, and the next day I was walking fragments; the broken parts left behind were precariously resting atop each other. Any sudden noise and I would have collapsed.

In Michoacán, one of my uncles always offered his bed when I visited. He would spend the night on the living room couch, he said. But when the lights went off, I heard his breathing becoming louder and louder until it was right next to my ear as he adjusted his body next to mine, spooning me. What began feeling like affection eventually turned into something painful, and he would cover my mouth with his hand that smelled of motor oil because he was a mechanic. At dinner he had complained that no matter how much he washed his hands, he couldn't get rid of the smell. And this many years later, neither have I.

How easy it was to move about that house in the cover of dark. The floors were concrete. Instead of doors, the bedrooms had curtains. Without bedsprings, the thick mattress didn't register movement, or the added weight of another body.

In the next bedroom, Abuela Herminia and Abuelo Melecio slept soundly. I wished I could have crawled out from under the blankets and slipped down to the floor like a puddle that spilled all the way to the foot of their bed. My mother's armoire stood at the far wall. She had left it here, along with all the furnishings in the kitchen, when we migrated to the U.S. A large plaster Jesus watched over the bed. Pinned to his cross, he couldn't help me now.

I would remember that Jesus, bound and useless, each time my older cousin in California woke me in the early hours. High on coke, he would turn on the radio to muffle my moans when he raped me. I was certain that the rest of the household would become suspicious, that the squeaking at 3 a.m. was too peculiar. I fantasized that one of the other seven people in the house would throw the door open and yank my cousin off me. At the same time, I was terrified of being discovered face down with my shorts around my ankles, as if I had willingly submitted to this violence. *Why didn't you fight back? Why did you let him? Did you like it?* It was better not to have to answer for anything. The assaults remained unspoken, even though I was certain they were not unheard. Not in that house where the sound of the refrigerator opening traveled down the hall, loud and clear.

Somebody had the munchies on one of those nights I was being assaulted. There was a piece of chocolate cake on the top shelf. I had come across it when I placed the jar of Kool-Aid back in the fridge during dinner. The cake was wrapped in tin foil. The unwrapping was slow and courteous as if that midnight prowler didn't want to wake anyone as they claimed the last piece of dessert. The foil was crushed into a ball and tossed into the trash bin. They missed the shot. The discarded foil struck the kitchen floor. The next day I would see it from the dining table. It was hidden from view just under the stove. One of my younger cousins opened the fridge and bent down to assess the contents.

"Did somebody eat the cake?" he asked.

I sat there quietly, unwilling to give away any information.

Later that afternoon, my older cousin winked at me from the rearview mirror as he drove me back to my grandparents' apartment. Another cousin rode in the front. I lay down in the back seat because I didn't want to be taunted anymore. He was so satisfied with himself, with the fact that, yet again, he had gotten away with it.

"Where's that water bottle?" my younger cousin asked.

My older cousin volunteered to grab it from the back. He reached over the seat and pretended to be searching. He forced his fingers up my shorts.

"Nothing here," he said.

We arrived at my grandparents' apartment in El Campo.

"Let us know if you want us to pick you up next weekend," he said. "You know where to find us."

My cousins laughed and left me standing there, the car becoming smaller and smaller as they drove away, and I imagined that I too was shrinking down to nothing for my assailant, who looked back at me through the rearview mirror. I imagined that he winked again.

And then there was my father's friend who always had something special for the schoolboy—a notebook, a fancy pen. He was allowed to walk into my bedroom to deliver that gift. He expected me to thank him with a hug. And then he grabbed me by the ass with one hand and with the other turned my head so that he could plant a sour kiss.

There was also that middle-aged neighbor who wandered over after I got back from school to ask my grandfather if I was free to help him fill out paperwork. He didn't read English. My grandfather asked me to go next door. I couldn't disobey this command. What was more innocent than helping a simple farmworker with a form? He offered me a soda. We filled out that piece of paper. He watched over my shoulder as I wrote the shaky letters on the lines. His breathing became heavier. The next time Abuelo sent me over, there was no paperwork to fill out. I recall thinking once that the man was not bad looking. The hairs on his chest showed through the white dress shirt he always wore. I might have called it sexy if I had known the word. When I finally got to feel those wiry hairs on my back, they burned. I mistook the sweat for bleeding and was sure that Abuelo would become infuriated when he saw the damage the neighbor had caused. But when I walked back home, Abuelo didn't say a word. I checked myself in the bathroom mirror. Where was the blood? I pulled down my shorts. Oh. There it was.

I had come to the conclusion that it was me who was tempting them somehow. My feminine mannerism drew them to me, and they stuck around when they realized I was one of those victims who wasn't going to say a word. We quiet ones were such a gift to their crimes. With us, their actions remained unknown, their reputations unsullied.

When I reached adolescence, I was no longer approached by my tormentors. Perhaps I had become too old and therefore undesirable. I wanted to believe that they had ceased seeking out their perverted pleasures, but I suspected that they hadn't, that they were now turning their attention to other boys and girls who were at that impressionable age when they could be shamed or threatened into silence.

"Don't tell anyone," they whispered. Sometimes softly, as if we were co-conspirators in these after-hours encounters. Or they spat the words out while they bit into my shoulders and neck, my eyes shut so tightly I saw flashes of light. Most of the time however, nothing was said. The act spoke for itself, or rather, it had no name or no words that I could take back to an adult to explain what had happened. One moment I'm lying down, ready to succumb to dreams, and the next I've been abducted, taken to a remote place in which everything around me was strange and unfamiliar.

Once, my younger cousins and I were playing in the deserted lot behind the apartment building in Thermal, where we all lived. The topsoil had hardened, and our favorite game was to sink our feet in, breaking through the salty crust. It made us feel powerful. We would create trails of jagged holes leading up to the dumping grounds, where we would turn over other people's trash, hoping to find anything we could call a treasure.

As we sifted through garbage with our feet, one of my cousins called out, "Quiet, everybody. There's a snake."

We froze where we stood, looking toward our surprise visitor laying like a discarded engine belt near the brush. We were alarmed but certain that if we remained motionless, we would not be attacked. And eventually, either because it was bored or because it simply resumed its search for better shade, it slithered away.

When those men climbed into my bed or entered my room or came close to me, I practiced that same stillness, knowing that eventually they were going to complete their task and then vanish into the same darkness from which they had emerged.

Not until I became an adult and finally disclosed this part of my childhood to other gay men did I realize we shared a horrible experience. Many of us had been molested.

"Predators can sniff out a vulnerable child in a crowd," my close friend explained to me. "Just feel lucky you survived, that you weren't killed or that you didn't kill yourself."

"So, we live with this all of our lives?" I asked naively.

"How else?"

"That doesn't seem fair," I said. "What do these pedophiles get to live with?"

"Well," my friend answered solemnly, "that's the fucked-up thing: they get to live with us."

The gravity of that statement sunk into my stomach. What he had said was true. These crimes against minors were not committed by creepy men driving by in a car, seducing us with ice cream or candy. They were executed by our very own family members. And what's more, in the González household, this was a family sickness.

I didn't know that then. And I'm not sure what solace I could have achieved with the knowledge that I wasn't the only one being groped, prodded, and sodomized. Of all the things that gave me strength to move out and move on with life at the age of seventeen, I gave very little power to the molestations. My only regret was believing that I had been the only victim.

Twelve years after leaving home, I reunited with one of my cousins, who had splintered off from the family as soon as she had her first child. She was driving, showing me around the city of Houston. Her two adolescent sons sat in the back seat, keeping themselves busy with their video games. She had moved to Texas some time ago for a fresh start and since I was on business in the area, we decided to connect.

"You know, you even sound like a Texan," I said. She laughed.

"You pick it up," she said.

Our conversation turned to the family we had both left behind. Neither of us had many pleasant things to say. I realized we were more than commiserating; we were justifying our actions, placing our respective isolations into a context that would keep us from ever dreaming of going back.

"I want my boys to grow up healthy," she said. "Not afraid that they're getting punished for any little thing, like Abuelo used to do."

I stared ahead at the downtown district, which looked cleaner than most downtowns. We passed a park that was having some kind of cultural gathering or event. Clearly Mexican. A large banner of la Virgen de Guadalupe flapped in the wind while underneath a line of patrons waited patiently in front of a raspado cart. A stage had been set up for a ballet folklórico performance. The dancers in their colorful Jalisco dresses stood at the foot of the stairs. The MC was making his remarks. I wanted to suggest to my cousin that maybe we should stop and see what this was all about, but she had complained about the hassle of downtown parking. Besides, we were on our way to visit her mother, whom I hadn't seen all these years.

"I think about it all the time," she continued. "And I've never stopped being angry about it. There was too much shit there. Puros mañosos."

Mañosos. I froze. One of the boys had put on his earphones and started singing along to whatever he was listening to. I focused my attention on the faint sounds of music coming through. Perhaps I could identify it without disrupting his reverie to ask.

"All of them," she said. Her tone had become stronger. "Even the ones you loved. I hate to tell you that but it's true."

I tried to look behind me from the corner of my eye to see if the boys were listening. They shouldn't hear this. But when my impulse was to press my finger to my lips, like Abuela, I began feeling nauseous.

"Hey," I said, my throat so dry I was about to start coughing.

We looked at each other. I wasn't sure how she was translating that "Hey." I wasn't sure about it myself. Was I telling her I didn't want to hear it or was I about to open the door to my secret as well? I stalled at the crossroads, holding back tears.

"I'm sorry," she said. "I just needed to get that off my chest. You're the only one from the past I can trust. I don't want to see or hear from anyone else."

I was so flustered I was no longer able to sight-see. I stared directly into the blinding glare of the windshield.

"And the women knew about them and didn't do anything about it," my cousin added. The women: our aunts, our mothers, Abuela.

By the time we reached our destination, I had disintegrated into the seat. During the visit, my aunt kept asking, "Why are you quiet? You must have something to say after all these years." But I was stuck so far back in the past that I wasn't sure how I was going to make it back to the present.

Twenty years after that, the daughter of another one of my cousins reached out through social media. She was in middle school the last time I saw her, but she had since separated herself from her parents and was now living outside the country with her husband.

"I'm much happier," she proclaimed.

Though when we made contact over the phone, she started rattling off a series of complaints about people that I had lost touch with decades ago. Very delicately, I told her as much.

"You have to learn to let them go," I said. "Otherwise, they won't let go of you."

"Easier said than done, tío," she said. She called me uncle as a title of respect because I was considerably older. "I won't forgive any of them. Ever."

I wasn't sure how to handle her rage. But I understood it. I didn't know how I had overcome mine either. I had discovered what triggered it: talking to the people of my past. Strolling through memory lane wasn't a pleasant experience. I regretted getting in touch with my niece, or my cousin in Texas. Abuela's hush finger flashed in my mind.

"You're away from home now," I said, trying to reassure her. "They can't do anything to you anymore."

"But what good is that if they're still in my head?" she said. "My poor mom. She's stuck there still. She told me what she had gone through. And I went through the same thing with my uncles, that bunch of mañosos."

My body grew cold. That word again. Whenever I heard it, I was reminded of the word "leña," which meant firewood. Chkári or iuikua in Purépecha, depending on the context. Indeed, my brain caught fire, consuming memories. I shut down.

"Hey, what's happening here?" she said. "You still with me or am I talking to dead air?"

"I'm here," I answered, too softly for her liking.

"You see? This is what I mean. None of you wants to talk about it. None of you wants to deal with it. That's why my mom can't even get out of bed sometimes. She just lays there, like a dead person, under the sheets while my little brothers and sisters run around trashing the house. It's like she gave up. I don't want to end up like her."

When my cousin in Texas told me about her experience, I wasn't ready. I couldn't put into words what los mañosos had done to me. I thought I had left that experience behind, or at least buried it deep enough so that it would take effort to dig it up again. Yet all it took to yank it out of the shadows was a single sentence, fierce as a claw hook. The truth looked as rotted and offensive as I remembered.

I thought that eventually I would get to that point of reckoning with my past. And when that time came, I would reach out to my cousin again, maybe fly down to Texas just to sit with her, face to face. I wanted her to see the same pain in me that I had seen in her. But then my cousin from Texas died, prematurely, leaving behind her two sons, and our conversation unfinished.

When I received word of her death, I thought selfishly, *What now? Was there anyone left to confide in?* And then the years passed by and people from my past died off or were forgotten, and I was able to bury that secret again. Until my niece drudged it up over the phone. Twenty years had passed, and I remained as unprepared as ever.

"I knew it was a mistake to tell you anything," she said.

I wanted to tell her that it wasn't. That I understood more than she knew. But I couldn't get the words out.

"Are you still there?" she asked.

"Yes," I said. My voice was even softer than before.

"I can barely hear you. Speak up! Speak up and tell me I'm not crazy! Tell me you believe what I'm telling you! Tell me I'll be alright!"

Before I could answer, she hung up. I tried calling her back right away but she wouldn't answer. I tried calling back an hour later. And the next day. Nothing. I knew it was hopeless. Whatever path we had traveled to find each other was gone. We were lost once more.

I called my brother in México. I told him about the call and what our niece had revealed, but I didn't tell him about my own experience.

"It's sad, Turrútut," he said, invoking the nickname we use with each other.

"Alex, listen," I said. "I know what she said is true. There were many ugly things happening in our family."

"What can we do about it now? Most of them are dead."

"But we're not. We're still in pain."

After a brief silence, I said, "Remember what I told you when your daughter was born? Remember that I told you never to leave her alone with *any* of the men in the family?"

"Yes," he said.

"That's why."

"I don't know what to say, Turrútut."

"Neither do I," I said. "I feel dizzy."

"What if she calls you again?" Alex had asked.

The thought filled me with dread.

We ended the call shortly after. Since we spoke once a week, I thought maybe together we could find those words to express this grief. But we didn't bring it up again. The world had become a different place during the pandemic. There were more pressing concerns and more urgent anxieties to deal with. Even the recent past seemed far away, let alone the days of our childhood, which we couldn't wait to flee.

Patron Saint of the Cupcake

Three. Three es tres. But for us it's tanímu.

—Abuela's lessons in Purépecha

IN MY TEENS, a frequent weekend pastime for my grandparents was hunting for yard sales. The attention-grabbing signs made it easy. Though sometimes we just happened upon the telltale spread on a lawn, compelling Abuelo to pull over immediately. Abuela liked picking at the second-hand clothes laid out on folding tables while Abuelo and I ruffled through the assortment of cardboard boxes on the driveway, containing everything from books to toys to tools. If there was a piece of used furniture, like an easy chair, we each took a turn sitting in it. Abuelo was also drawn to lamps and kitchen electronics, though I rarely saw him take one of them home. Abuela bought a shirt or a sweater once in a while, but for him this was strictly an activity to kill time on a Sunday morning.

Tía Melania also loved yard sales. When she had me tag along, it was because she wanted a translator. Her children refused to be seen in such a place by anyone they knew. I didn't care. I didn't consider any of my classmates in junior high friends. And not once did I ever run into anyone I recognized.

Las ventas, my family called them. Someone's garage had exploded and the patrons swooped in like crows to pick through the detritus.

I didn't cringe at the thought of wearing someone else's worn shoes or putting on a shirt with a small stain that had made it unwearable to its original owner. We couldn't afford new things unless we bought them across the border in Mexicali. But Mexican clothing was so distinct from what the

68

American kids wore that these new items looked foreign and out of fashion. The California flea markets sold new clothes, but they were cheap-looking because they were mass produced in China. There was no winning the game of style, so I stopped caring about it, even if the other kids in school made fun of me.

For Christmas one year, Tía Melania gave my brother and me knitted wool sweaters from the flea market. His was tan with black designs woven into a pattern that circled the torso and sleeves. Mine was identical, except it was white. When school resumed after winter break, the weather was still cool in the mornings. I wore that sweater regularly because it was the warmest one I owned. My brother, on the other hand, refused to wear it even once.

"I'm not wearing no damn Charlie Brown clothes," he said.

When I walked into science class, I heard someone whistling the theme song to *The Flintstones*. I thought nothing of it, until I realized that it had to be more than a passing coincidence that I heard this each time I walked into the classroom that winter. Eventually others caught on and joined in the laughter until the science teacher quieted everyone down.

I might have felt more humiliated if I cared about any of them. But I didn't. I refused to speak to anyone or to hang out with them during free period or during lunch. I would rather hide out in the library and read, a habit I kept through high school.

Being poor wasn't foreign in El Campo, where we were surrounded by other families who also worked in the agricultural fields. I didn't think there was anything to be ashamed of. Besides, I admired Tía Melania's zeal and Abuela's concentration as they sifted through other people's castoffs.

The sellers were not the only enterprising people present at these yard sales. Once in a while, a small lemonade or cupcake stand sat a few feet apart from the chaos. A young girl or two stood behind a homemade sign that read: *50¢ a cup* or *50¢ a piece*. Without fail, Abuela would walk over to make a purchase.

At first, I didn't take much notice, though I was surprised Abuela didn't offer to buy me a brownie or a refreshing cup of lemonade. She stood there next to the ragtag stand as she enjoyed her treat. Once she bought a cupcake just before we climbed back in the car, and she sat calmly in her seat, savoring it. The smell wafted to the back, where I sat, feeling left out. I had spent what little change I had on a book and a deck of cards. I stared down at my items and tried not to think about the sugar high Abuela was enjoying all the way home.

The next time we stopped at a yard sale, I kept my eye on the nearby stand touting chocolate chip cookies. I wasn't compelled to spend my money on a treat made by a child younger than me. But that didn't stop Abuela. After having her fill of browsing through used clothing, she beelined it to the stand and pulled out a dollar from her bag. The little blonde girl looked delighted as she gave my grandmother two quarters back since each cookie was twenty-five cents. Still, Abuela ate them both.

I began to wonder about this selfish quirk. Abuelo had a similar one with seafood. Because of our mother's death and our father's abandonment, my brother and I qualified for government assistance after we moved in with our grandparents. Each month we received a check administered by Abuelo, yet we received no personal allowance since, in his view, we had no personal expenses.

When that check arrived, my grandparents took a long trip to the grocery store and came back fully stocked with the essentials—bread, rice, beans, veggies, cereals, milk. I never imagined there was money to splurge on anything special, until I stumbled upon Abuelo's little guilty pleasures in the freezer.

I didn't have many occasions to look in the top compartment of the refrigerator. But one afternoon I bumped my elbow against the door and Abuela suggested I put ice on it. I opened the freezer door and reached into the tray for ice cubes. Something strange caught my eye. It was sealed in plastic with a price label on it, clearly an item from the market. It looked like a rock. Upon closer inspection, I discovered it was a large clam, nothing like the three-inch mussels we fished out of the dirty canals across the border. I also found a pair of octopus tentacles, tilapia, and shrimp. Except for the fish, none of the other items had ever been served at dinner. Nor had I seen Abuelo cook them for himself. But they were his treasure, I was sure of it. I imagined he prepared these delicacies while Abuela was out laboring in the packinghouse and I was at school.

I didn't ask anyone about this because I wasn't that interested. Like Abuela's yard sale cupcakes, seafood wasn't appetizing to me. Though I did figure out that he was buying these items with the extra funds he received for becoming his grandsons' legal guardian. It made sense suddenly why Abuelo became furious when my brother, Alex, dropped out of school and insisted on moving in with our father in Mexicali. His monthly check would be cut in half.

"You better not go down that same road!" he yelled at me as I sat at the dining table, doing my homework.

I must have looked frightened because Abuela stepped forward right away and tried to calm him down, assuring him that I liked school, even though I had never expressed that to her. In fact, neither of them had ever asked or bothered to look at my grades. And I certainly didn't volunteer any progress reports.

We lived together, but I didn't feel close to them. I would recognize this type of housing environment once I got to college and rented apartments with roommates: each person kept to their own interests and their own secrets. It didn't make sense to be emotionally detached from family, especially one's grandparents, but that's how we cohabitated until I left for the university.

We did, however, do one thing together: go to yard sales, where I got to spend the few dollars my father gave me when he dropped in to visit his parents, which was not often. He had remarried and Abuelo wasn't particularly fond of his new wife or their three rowdy boys. My father understood this. He walked in alone and left unceremoniously an hour or so later. I knew he wasn't there to visit me because we hardly spoke. I felt like an afterthought at times because he would rush into my bedroom just before leaving to offer me what I believed to be a consolation prize. I took the spending money anyway. Abuelo was right: I didn't have any personal expenses, except for books, the one thing that made me happy.

A used book had a very different history than used shorts or a used blender. The only property that wore off was its newness, but its magic remained intact. Unlike other used items, books were not being discarded— they were being shared. Its secondhand status was not a downgrade but a seal of approval. Dog-eared pages, underlined sentences, highlighted passages, even small notes on the margins were all evidence of its ability to hold a reader's interest. Such books called to me. When I held them in my hands, I understood what a sacred gift I was touching: somebody else's eyes had spent hours tracing every single word, and that pleasure had now been entrusted to me.

I came to understand that a similar euphoria seized Abuela when she walked over to the cupcake stand. She did have a sweet tooth, much needier than mine. During Halloween season, she made sure to buy plenty of candies for the treat-or-treaters, but she was actually stingy with her giveaways. Abuelo would chastise her for sitting outside well into the night, waiting for the costumed children to walk up with their paper bags or plastic pumpkins. Abuela was committed to seeing the evening through, keeping herself occupied by unwrapping a caramel every so often. I could hear the crinkling of the plastic wrapper through the bedroom window, and though she didn't make any sounds of satisfaction, I knew she was in her private heaven. After Halloween, there was plenty of candy left over, enough for her to enjoy the rest of November.

"Why didn't you give all that garbage away?" Abuelo complained because the excess bags of candy took up room in the cupboards. Since we had a small kitchen, space was precious.

Abuela held one finger up. "One child, one candy," she said firmly.

I couldn't help but grin. She mirrored my expression as she unwrapped a piece of candy. She popped the red-and-white starlight mint into her mouth with gusto.

My curiosity about her yard sale stand patronage didn't wane, however. I suspected it was more than just reaching for something sweet. But I didn't want to disrupt her reverie as she enjoyed yet another cupcake, this one with lemon frosting and sprinkles. Abuelo, however, broached the subject. He was in a particularly foul mood that morning because the car was making funny noises all the way to the yard sale. His exasperation was triggered again when he restarted the engine as we prepared to go home. The strange noise had gotten worse. Abuela's cutesy little cupcake didn't sync with the moment.

"Ay, Maruca," he said. "What's so great about these tiny crumbs of bread? Are you sure they're not store-bought?"

Undeterred, Abuela bit into her cupcake. When she turned to Abuelo, I noticed a green sprinkle stuck to her upper lip, but I didn't bother to point it out since I knew she would run her tongue across it like a cat signaling it had been sated.

When the car kept rattling, Abuelo redirected his energy.

"This piece of shit," he said. "I should roll it into the Salton Sea."

I pictured Abuelo driving down to the man-made lake in the middle of the Coachella Valley desert and wondered if there was enough water left to submerge an entire car.

Later that afternoon, taking advantage of the fact that Abuelo had gone to consult a mechanic, I sat next to Abuela as she rummaged through her basket of jewelry. Beneath the clutter of earrings, she kept a sizeable collection of fake precious stones. She would dig into them and then let them rain back into the basket. This must have been meditative for her because she performed this action repeatedly before she continued on her quest for a ring or earrings that sparkled in the light.

I never asked Abuela where and how she had acquired her collection because one thing was certain: she didn't add to it. At the yard sales, she might glance over at the table with costume jewelry spread out on a cloth or dangling from an earring tree, but these displays rarely called to her like the heaps of clothing. It seemed odd suddenly because over the years, I had witnessed countless times how she became entranced with her stones.

When she paused her sifting, I cut in with my question.

"Abuela," I said. "You really do like those cupcakes at the yard sales, don't you?"

Another thought popped into my head. When she went grocery shopping, she didn't bring back any cupcakes, though she returned with a generous helping of fruit Danish covered in swirls of frosting. Or coconut cake, which she basically enjoyed by herself because neither Abuelo nor I appreciated that flavor. Yet there she was at the yard sales, moving in methodically toward the cupcake stand. It was as if she had established a clear boundary between what she enjoyed inside the house and outside. At least with cupcakes and jewelry.

"They're good," she said. She smiled. She had forgotten or hadn't bothered to insert her dentures. That smile was mostly gums.

"And what else?" I said, hoping to coax a better answer.

"I like them," she added, grinning.

Abuela knew what I was after. She proceeded to tell me a story while looking through the items in the basket.

"When I was a girl, I wanted to make my own money. But who was going to give a job to a child who wasn't even wearing shoes?"

The detail about walking about barefoot in Nahuatzen stayed with me. It wasn't the first time she had mentioned it. Each time my throat tightened.

"I had almost given up when I came across the sweet potato seller. She had a large tub of sweet potatoes she was cleaning and cutting before cooking them over the fire. But people started arriving and she became flustered. Well, I saw an opportunity."

Abuela's eyes brightened. This happened when she was particularly pleased with herself.

"Since I was the only one offering to help, she had to accept. She had no choice, even though I was young. But I knew how to cut since Mamá Lola insisted I had to learn early. Well, there I was, washing and cutting until she ran out of sweet potatoes."

She paused. I knew about this pause. Abuelo did it, and so did my father, Tía Melania, and Tío Rafa. Whenever they were storytelling, they inserted these silences for dramatic effect. Tía Melania was the master of the craft, however, because she insisted on telling her tale while eating a taco or spooning menudo into her mouth. The pause was an opportunity to take the next bite or spoonful of stew. Once we caught on, we still weren't certain what was being embedded into what: the story into the meal or the meal into the story. A relative who was an academic in Seattle called it "the storytelling of the people, the working poor." This included the Purépecha. I had heard Indigenous storytellers spin a tale the same way, with long, drawn-out pauses and a pace that drew the audience into rapt attention.

Abuela continued: "The crowd at the corner began to disperse as soon as they noticed the seller scooping the last bits of sweet potato into a cup and tipping the pot to let the final traces of molasses water pour out. My hands were raw and achy by then, but I made it through the entire tub."

She shook her head, signaling that the story was about to take a twist.

"I stood there as the woman started getting her things together. She went about her business as if she had forgotten all about me. I said to her, 'Señora, are you going to pay me for the work I did?' When she turned around, she looked offended. 'But you asked if you could help,' she said. 'You offered to do me a favor.'"

Abuela shook her head and sighed.

"A favor. Can you imagine that? I stood there for hours with the expectation that I was earning money for the first time. I had already planned how I was going to enter the house, bragging to my sisters that I had pesos to spend. And this chingada vieja cheated me of that."

"What did you do?" I asked.

"What could I do? I was still a stupid girl. I knew how to slice a vegetable but not how to argue. I walked home and didn't tell anybody because they would blame me, not the grown-up who had outsmarted me."

One thing about the storytelling of the people was that it didn't give away the moral of the story. Storytelling was a holistic experience, not always a build-up to a lesson. It was up to the listener to take some of what had been offered and digest it according to their needs. As for the connection between this travesty of the sweet potato seller and the cupcake stands, I had been focusing on the wrong image. It wasn't the cupcake I had to wonder about, or even Abuela as she stood at the stand, exchanging pocket change for a treat. It was the beaming girls themselves. How they lit up when they saw a customer approaching, how they bared their baby teeth and gap-toothed smiles with glee. Abuela was the woman who took them seriously, patronizing their businesses and demonstrating her gratitude when she savored the cupcake in front of them. It was too easy to dismiss these girls or keep them invisible, and so rewarding to let them know they had been seen.

The next time we dropped in on a yard sale with a cupcake stand, I felt sentimental about the insider knowledge of Abuela's actions. When she walked to a small table with a modest display of baked treats, I turned my entire body around to face the scene as if that made me a participant somehow. The young girl sitting behind the table stood up and, despite the language barrier, was able to communicate with my grandmother, who picked up a chocolate cupcake whose frosting glimmered in the sun. Abuela took a small bite and nodded in approval, delighting the young seller. When she headed back to the sales items, I started walking in her direction. I wanted to let her know that I understood now and that I too found joy in her kindness toward these girls who wanted to earn a little extra spending money—money that had more value because they had worked for it. But as I got closer to Abuela, I realized she was lost in a state of bliss, her eyes looking out into space as she took another bite of her cupcake. I stopped and remained silent as she passed me by as gracefully as a leaf stirred into the air by a gentle wind.

SECOND INTERLUDE

Adolescence with a Wall in It

Two women are walking alongside the border wall between Mexicali and Calexico. This is California in the early 1980s, when the wall was made of vertical bars, like a cage. Long before it was covered with wire. Long before it became a barrier of metal sheets that no one could see through. The bars were close together, just like the one at the Mexicali zoo that kept the old lion from squeezing through. There was no fear of the lion actually attacking anyone because it had no teeth. Or claws. Or muscle. But the zookeepers were afraid that if it escaped into the streets, the hungry stray dogs would have their way with it. Therefore, the cage was for the lion's protection, not for us kids who kept trying to make it roar by yelling or tossing empty cartons of juice at it. The old lion simply yawned and stared right through us with disinterest. When Tía Melania craned her neck to inspect it more closely, she said with certainty, "That animal has cataracts."

Tía Melania is one of those two women. The other is Irene. Irene called Tía Melania her mother-in-law even though she wasn't married to any of my cousins. Irene was a funny lady with a funny walk: she would swing her arms so wildly that the joke was that even the cars passing her by on the street had to veer slightly to the side to avoid getting struck.

When my brother, Alex, and I spent our summers at Tía Melania's house in Mexicali, she had two more mouths to feed. And our job, since we were U.S. citizens, was to cross the border to buy groceries on the American side.

The sales signs screamed right through the bars, tempting the Mexican customers with local passports to cross over and buy bread, chicken, bologna, hot dogs—all the things my brother and I would carry back. My cousin Marcial came along, but only because he could use Tía Melania's local passport, which was permissible back in the day. Alex and I, barely adolescents, pulled out our black-and-white birth certificates that the border guards only glanced at before allowing us through. If we were asked, "What's the purpose of your trip?" Cousin Marcial, always the joker, would answer, "Weenies." It always got a chuckle out of the guards.

The three of us would cross back and forth two times and Tía Melania would wait on the Mexican side with our older cousin to collect the groceries. If we were lucky, Tío Juve might come by in the truck. But we were rarely lucky because this was the era before cell phones, and pay phones were usually broken or busy with lines of people waiting to contact someone because they had been deported or not allowed to cross. Since I was Tía Melania's favorite, she would ask me to accompany her to the corner to make a call. Alex and Marcial had to wait against the wall with the paper bags of groceries gathered at their feet.

Waiting in that line was a somber affair. I marveled at how a person stood there patiently, quietly, until it was their turn to pick up the receiver. If no one answered, they sighed and walked to the end of the long line to try again later. Or they would walk away, dispirited. It was a sad thing not to be able to reach anyone on the other end of the line. If it was a young man, he would look away, his face turned to the busy street and his body slowly dissolved into the crowds. If it was a young woman, which was rare, she would look back at the rest of us, distress quite visible on her face, so much so that our own faces would mirror it, and maybe someone offered words of encouragement, like "Ánimo, hija." That word, "hija," was kind, but it lingered in the air for only a moment before it dropped to the ground like the cartons of juice jettisoned toward the lion.

If someone did answer the call, the conversation got loud and began with a colorful expression like "The motherfuckers threw me out!" or it remained hushed, an exchange of whispers in a shaky voice that escalated into anger or anguish, and then silence again. Sometimes those men left dejected or bored and then sat down with their backs against the bars. Alex and Marcial stood there, watching over the groceries, instructed not to give anyone a piece of bread or a slice of bologna no matter how much they begged. "You start feeding one, you have to feed them all," is all Tía Melania would say. She was not an unsympathetic woman, just not a charitable one. Besides, there were all those mouths to feed: her husband's, her five children's, Alex's, mine.

For us, the phone call was a different matter. If we reached my uncle, we were overjoyed. He would arrive less than an hour later and we would wait for him at our usual meeting spot, a Chinese restaurant with a big yellow sign with Chinese characters. Its name, Chung Hua, was unforgettable because that's what we called every Chinese restaurant. "I want to eat at the Chung Hua," my younger cousins said. "Oh, look, there's a Chung Hua," they would point out while we sat in the back of my uncle's truck on our way to this place or that.

To get to the Chung Hua with the bags of groceries in our arms, we would have to pass the cantinas. Our sweaty arms dampened the paper bags and there was nothing to do but hope they wouldn't soak through. Alex and Marcial would giggle and elbow each other because our older cousin once pointed out that these cantinas were brothels. They called every brothel a Gato Negro. I knew Tía Melania disapproved. I walked looking straight ahead, ignoring the buildings of ill-repute with their music and laughter and pretty ladies with bright-red lipstick standing outside the entrances. There was no avoiding this street without adding more distance to our meeting spot.

Once, a woman caught my eye because she looked beautiful to me in her bright makeup and tight black blouse and shiny skirt. She wasn't making eye contact with anyone even though many people walking by stared at her. She didn't smile. She was simply looking out into the polluted air as if lost in thought. My mother had just died the year before. I had adopted the strange habit of making women who looked lovely and lonely my mothers. This woman was quite different from my mother, who was short and plump and wore no makeup, but I couldn't resist fantasizing that she would suddenly see me and recognize me and offer me an affectionate smile, just like my mother used to do when I came home from school. The pretty woman in front of the Gato Negro didn't even notice me, but I was grateful anyway because she had given me a moment of solace from my sadness.

Reaching my uncle by phone didn't happen often. He was an electrician and on demand, even on the weekends. My cousin Mari, the only female in our cluster of mouths to feed, would deliver the bad news over the phone, which irritated my aunt because we were going to have to take the bus. No one liked the bus, especially not in the summer while carrying groceries, because the buses were crowded and the bread, warm from all that time in the heat, was easily crushed, and we would have to spread jam on slices shaped like rectangles instead of squares, which somehow made it feel that we were getting less food.

Tía Melania always taught us to offer our seats to the ladies while on a bus. But she didn't scold us if we found a seat and remained seated if we had bags of groceries on our laps. We had been carrying them all the way from the other side of the border. The old bus would shake with the potholes and jump with the speed bumps; all the passengers' bodies swayed side to side and it was always a joke to Alex and Marcial but not to me because the motion made me queasy.

When we got home, it was my cousin Mari's job to put everything away. Tía Melania was overprotective of Mari, who had to stay at home to do the cleaning. When I remember her, I think about her face looking out from the kitchen window that overlooked the street. If I had to make a quick run to the tiny store down the block, I glanced back at her as she washed the dishes or stood over the stove, since she also did most of the cooking. If the window was open, there was still a screen, and she would try to splash water at me while I passed beneath it and I would shriek even if only one drop managed to reach me because it made her smile.

Mari was my favorite cousin. But she was the only girl. We had a second female cousin who spent the summer with us once in a while, but she was all tomboy and much too young to want to sit next to Mari on the sidewalk to wonder about the world in the evenings after the chores got done. Mari was not allowed to wander away from the house even though she was a few years older than me. And at sundown she had to go into her room. I was the only one of the boys allowed to sleep on the floor next to her bed. We would ask each other to recite the different prayers in the dark.

"El credo," she whispered. And I would whisper the Apostles' creed.

"Anima Christi," I would whisper. And she would whisper the litany.

The point was to drift off into sleep at the same time. The point was to escape into dream.

By the time I woke up in the morning, Mari was already up and moving pans in the kitchen to make breakfast for the entire household. The bacon started to fry, the pot of beans left soaking overnight was already boiling, and the tortillas were getting stacked in a small basket and covered with cloth to keep them warm until the rest of us gathered around the dining table to eat.

I waited until the very end to join Mari as she nibbled on the small portions of what she had made. In the meantime, I stayed wrapped in the blanket a bit longer, looking under Mari's bed, where she kept her treasures: magazines her mother read first, fotonovelas she traded with the neighbor through the fence, and a box of hair clips and earrings. The clips and earrings had been smuggled into the house by me.

After it became routine for Alex, Marcial, and me to cross the border each week, Mari broke our nightly ritual to inquire about that experience.

"What other kinds of stores do you walk by?" she asked.

Surprised by the question, I had to concentrate because in truth I hadn't paid much attention.

"Shops, I guess," I said. "Like clothing stores. Toy stores."

"How about beauty supply stores?"

"I don't know," I said. "I can't remember."

"When you're on the other side, look for them."

"Okay," I said. Then I whispered, "Ave María," because I didn't want to neglect our prayers.

The next time I crossed into Calexico, I saw the street a bit differently. Somehow it was more alive, perhaps because I was now more aware. Yes, there was a beauty supply store, and a barbershop and hair salon, a jewelry store, a bus station, and a number of fast-food restaurants buzzing with customers. And, oh, there on the corner was an American Chung Hua.

When we returned home, I gave Mari a full report. She nodded without saying a word. But the night before the next trip, she slipped me five one-dollar bills in the dark.

"Buy me something," she said. "From the other side."

I was more surprised by the money than the request. I didn't want to ask where she had gotten the dollar bills because none of us received an allowance. When the paletero walked by, ringing that familiar bell, we had to beg for change before we ran out the door to catch up to him.

"What do you want me to buy?"

"Hair clips," she said. "And pretty earrings. Maybe a lipstick. Whatever you can get with five dollars."

"But I don't know anything about girl things," I said.

"It doesn't matter," she said. "Just bring me pretty things. From the other side."

I didn't worry too much about how I was going to get away from Alex and Marcial; they were easy to manipulate at that age. As we walked down the street on our way to the grocery store, I made a rebellious suggestion.

"Hey," I said. "How about we go to the toy store for a few minutes before going to the market?"

It didn't take much convincing. The lines at the checkout were unpredictable. Sometimes they were tedious and long; other times they moved efficiently. If we took a little longer getting the groceries, Tía Melania would never suspect a thing.

That's how I was able to break off from the other two to buy Mari's pretty things. The boys were too distracted trying out the toy guns and action figures. Every week after that, we did the same thing. While they horsed around, I picked out clips shaped like butterflies, colorful ribbons and silky bows, plastic bracelets, and tiny earrings that glared in the light. As much as I could hide in my pockets. I was hesitant to buy lipstick because it was already uncomfortable enough watching the puzzled look on the cashier's face when I dropped the girly items on the counter. But after a few weeks, she became indifferent, and I tossed a stick of glittery lip gloss into the mix.

Mari never really wore the things I brought her, except maybe the tiny earrings, which she could keep hidden beneath her hair. We both knew this was contraband. Instead, on those days where I couldn't resist joining the others in a game of freeze tag or hide and seek, Mari hid in her room and sifted through a shoebox cluttered with her pretty things. I discovered it when I woke up one morning and saw it there, tucked away in the shadows under the bed. After peaking in, I immediately shoved the box back in because this was the only thing that was hers alone, and I had no right to touch it. Her secret was safe with me.

Everything was moving along as usual one morning before our weekly trip to Calexico. And then suddenly the plan started to fall apart. Tío Juve received a call about an emergency job. He was the best electrician in the area. He had to go. But he needed his apprentices with him for support. That meant that our cousins would not be available to help carry the groceries.

"That's all fine and good," Tía Melania said. "But now what?"

"Why don't you ask the neighbor's son," my uncle suggested, and that made my aunt cringe.

"He's useless. I might as well go alone," she snapped.

"Well, you figure it out. I need to get to work," my uncle said as he walked away, calling out to our cousins, who were watching TV in the living room.

We sat around the kitchen as Tía Melania pondered. That's when Mari, who usually didn't say anything, stepped out of her silence.

"I can go," she suggested.

The air changed in that moment. Tía Melania's expression went from anxious to angry.

"You must be crazy," she said. "With all those perverted men on the streets, and all those desperate wetbacks that have nothing to do once they get deported but get drunk and walk about like fumigated spiders! Absolutely not."

Mari didn't show any emotion, but I knew she was dismayed. She remained silent and accepted the reality of her imprisonment. The tension, however, didn't linger long because all of a sudden, Irene burst in through the door.

Tía Melania was overjoyed for once at the unexpected arrival of her arm-swinging make-believe daughter-in-law. "Irene!" she squealed. "Guess where we're going?"

I was actually stunned that my aunt's determination to keep Mari locked up was so staunch that she would rather take a woman who was not really all there, to be honest. Irene said one silly thing after another and made us laugh because we knew she wasn't trying to. That was just the way she was. We didn't laugh with her most of the time; we laughed at her. And Tía Melania loved to coax it out.

"Irene," my aunt said one time. "I hate to tell you this, but I think your husband's cheating on you."

"Ay, suegra," Irene replied. "He's your son, I have to love him no matter what. And besides, I'm not a jealous wife."

"But what if he leaves you?"

"Then I'll love him even more. All I can do is call to him like Mrs. Goat calls out to Mr. Goat."

"And how is that?"

"She sticks her head out the door and yells, 'Come baaaaaaaaack!'"

In any case, that's how Irene ended up joining us on that trip. As we walked out the door, I looked back at Mari, whose body seemed to be pulsing with pain. When Tía Melania sifted through her purse for our bus fare, I realized then where Mari was getting the money from. It was a sin to steal. The dollar bills Mari had given me the night before felt hot in my pocket. But I didn't care. It was our way to protest this injustice.

On the bus trip to the border, Irene was saying her usual nonsense, keeping Tía Melania and even the other passengers amused the whole way and distracted from the heat and stuffiness. I listened but couldn't laugh along, picturing Mari watching us leave from behind the window screen.

As we walked along the wall toward the line of border crossers, Tía Melania and Irene stayed a few steps ahead of Alex and me. Irene swung her arms as usual.

"Oh, suegra," Irene said. "One day I hope to go to the other side. It must be very magical."

"Oh, it is," Tía Melania said. "Everything is much better on the other side. They have better cars and better food."

"How wonderful!"

I scowled at my aunt's exaggerations. But as we walked past the men who had been deported or denied entry, at the long line of people waiting to cross, at the long line of people waiting to make a lifesaving call, at the long lines of cars crawling toward the checkpoint, everything and everyone moving arduously slow, I realized that Mexicans wanted to believe all those things were true, otherwise the sacrifice and heartache weren't worth it. It had to be better in order to aspire to it. Wasn't that what my parents had done? Hadn't they made sure that Alex and I were born on the other side so that we didn't have to suffer to attain what many wanted?

I was born a U.S. citizen. Just like I had been born a male. What strange luck was mine to have these privileges and freedoms.

"In fact," Tía Melania said, "they say that it's not as hot over there as it is here."

Irene paused for a moment. She stuck her arm through the bars and declared, "Oh, suegra, you're absolutely right! It *is* much cooler on the other side!"

Sounds at Night

Uíchu es perro es dog. Guau guau. Uíchu.

—Abuela's lessons in Purépecha

WE ALL KNEW. Did anyone do anything about it? Say anything? Did Abuelo change or did he just get better at hiding it? The few times I saw my grand-parents arguing, the exchange lasted less than a few minutes, ending with a grunt or a sigh that sounded so conclusive that I suspected the conflict was not going to be picked up again. In fact, the tension dropped so suddenly that it wasn't odd for them to simply switch to a less emotional tone as if walking from one room to another. If anything, I remember them bantering light-heartedly more often than I remember them quarreling. In this decades-long marriage, their dynamic, at least in the open, was shaped by humor.

"Maruca," Abuelo called out. "Get me a clean shirt."

Abuela returned from their bedroom with a tank top.

"Now why did you bring this one? It's too loose," he protested. "It's a better fit for the refrigerator."

Abuelo chuckled at his own joke, but Abuela wasn't going to give him the last word.

"Don't say that, Perrillo," she said with a mischievous grin, because I was her audience in that moment. "The refrigerator's been the same size since we moved in. It hasn't stretched out the kitchen one bit."

Abuelo paused to think about that, and when it finally sank in, he joined Abuela's laughter.

I laughed as well, though I waited for Abuelo to signal that permission. I had learned as a child not to anger or upset him. Even though I was a teenager, able to defend myself should he ever try to hit me again, I was still fearful and didn't tempt fate.

Abuela seemed brave with her jabs, but maybe she had learned a long time ago when it was safe to press her luck. Around Abuelo we were usually docile and reserved. When he burst into complaint about something or someone, we knew not to make any sudden moves. Or rather, my body knew. The tantrum was a signal to freeze because the mind was recollecting all those times Abuelo unleashed his rage with a belt, the broom handle, a piece of wire, a leather strap, his ankle boot, his bare foot, the soup ladle, a small can of tomato soup.

During my high school years, living in that two-bedroom apartment in El Campo that was too small to keep secrets, I don't recall seeing or hearing anything that would have indicated to me that the physical abuse had continued. I surmised that just as he had promised my father that he would not lay a hand on my brother and me again, he made that same promise about Abuela. But whether or not that was true, the harm had already been done. Each strike or kick, and the pain that followed, was committed to memory.

When we first crossed the border and all four families lived in one apartment, there were plenty of beatings. No one was spared. If Abuelo didn't hit me, then one of my older cousins did. Or Tía Melania, who had become the designated disciplinarian because she didn't ask questions when one of us kids got in trouble and the finger-pointing started. She hit all of us at once. The older cousins were always luckier because they weren't afraid to flee the scene. I, on the other hand, stood paralyzed, waiting for the blow.

"It's going to be worse for you if you run!" she threatened as she chased those who had dared escape their punishment.

My cousin Mari would inevitably whisper in my ear, "Do you see how she hits me the hardest?"

That claim was made by many members of the household: *I have it worse than any of you. I get it worse than the rest of you.* I am not sure what was achieved by this odd competition for most aggrieved. We all lived under the same roof, we all ate the same watered-down stews and received the same rations of meat. Abuelo was not crueler to any one person than he was with the rest. He favored humiliating the grow-ups verbally, but the grandchildren got the leather strap that hung ominously from the wall, so visible and convenient to point to when he wanted to issue a warning.

That leather strap was used on horses to get them to pick up speed. I had seen the men traveling down from the mountains of Michoacán many times. The loud clip-clopping of the horseshoes on cobblestone called me out. Horsemen looked as majestic as the Magi, slowly descending with a pile of chopped wood or a cluster of branches resting on the animal's rump. When a horse hesitated, the rider gave it an encouraging slap on the flank with the leather strap, which startled the horse into action. But it wasn't a violent gesture. When the horseman puckered his lips and made a kissing sound, it seemed to reassure the horse that his master wasn't expressing anger. The parade turned the corner eventually, leaving behind a trail of droppings that steamed during cold weather and drew large flies that sparkled green or blue in the hot sun.

The strap in Abuelo's hands didn't offer any beauty or grace. He wielded it about awkwardly yet triumphantly because that object in his hand warranted more fear and respect than he did.

If the strap wasn't handy, he resorted to kicking—a labored reflex that surprised the recipient because it came without warning from behind. When he kicked the other kids, I thought it looked slightly comical, as if he really didn't know how to kick. It was more like a shove. But when he kicked me, I understood that it was less an act of physical aggression and more an act of humiliation. Stray dogs got kicked. And so did stubborn doors that wouldn't open. It was rejection, a statement of repugnance, and a devaluing of one's worth.

There was no quick recovery from attacks of the psyche. The grief of feeling worthless stuck with me throughout the night. I wanted to hide inside the dark forever because the next day I would be reminded of that kick each time I heard Abuelo's hairy foot shuffling about.

And then there were the beatings we heard at night, under the cover of darkness, that paralyzed the entire household. The apartment became still, as if we were all holding our breaths in our beds. These were not discussed in the open, not in front of the children anyway, though sometimes we discussed them among ourselves.

"Someone was getting their ass creamed last night," my oldest cousin said. "It was either Tía Marta or Abuela."

"Let's hope it was Tía Marta," another said. "I don't want to imagine someone hitting Abuela."

"Someone? You mean Abuelo. Who else would hit her?"

This opened the door to a collective hatred of Abuelo.

"I can't wait to get bigger," my cousin said. "I'm going to hit him back."

The rest of us recoiled at that notion, looking around us as if this wish might guarantee another beating.

"Fuck, look at this," my cousin said. He raised his shorts to show the square-shaped mark the strap had left. I recognized that bruise. I had seen it many times on my own legs and arms.

The mornings after those late-night beatings, the adults sat poker-faced at breakfast, though they spoke in softer decibels. The unspoken lingered in the air and we kids knew better than to ask. If they didn't want to give this violence language, we certainly weren't going to look for it.

Only once did anyone dare name what was happening and to whom. It was Tío Ramón, always the most rebellious because he was the youngest of Abuela's children. He was on a plane all his own in that household because he was the only single adult, but much younger than his married siblings. He was also much older than all his nieces and nephews. He was the only one spared of any physical punishments. This allotted him a level of permission to be outspoken when he wanted to be.

One morning, after yet another late-night occurrence, he broke the code of silence. The adults had gathered around the table. The kids were allowed to take their plates into the living room to watch television while we ate on the floor. I finished my meal. I walked back into the kitchen to leave the plate in the sink.

"I don't understand why no one says anything," he said.

No one responded. Not my father or mother. Not my aunts or uncle.

"There's no reason for it," he added.

Still no one spoke.

"I just want to get the hell out of this house. I want to get away from all you cowards."

"It's not as easy as it seems," my father said. "You'll see."

"What I see is my father gets to do whatever he wants around here like he's king. Why don't you confront him? Why don't you stop him from beating your kids? From beating my mother?"

He was speaking to his two older brothers. My father and Tío Rafa kept eating, undeterred.

When Abuelo and Abuela finally stepped out of their bedroom, I thought that Tío Ramón had finally mustered the courage to confront Abuelo himself. I stood by the sink in anticipation. I didn't want to miss Abuelo getting his comeuppance.

Abuela stepped into the kitchen slowly, but Abuelo walked to the bathroom. The adults around the table began to disperse; only Tío Ramón stayed behind because it was Abuela who prepared his breakfast: an egg, sunnyside up. As usual he would eat only the yolk with a piece of bread and leave the whites to whomever wanted to take it.

"How did you sleep, Amá?" he asked Abuela.

"I slept well, mi niño," she said. She still called him her niño even though there was no boy left in Tío Ramón's body.

He walked up behind her as she prepared his egg. He began to rub her shoulders and then wrapped his arms around her as he lowered his head to kiss her cheek. The expression of affection disconcerted me. We didn't do those things in this family. Just like it dawned on me many years later that I never once heard any of the married couples having sex. Either they were extremely quiet or such an activity was just impossible in an apartment full of people and twice as many headaches.

Abuela understood the special moment as well. She didn't have to turn around for me to sense that she had become emotional. I felt as if I was encroaching. I backed away, looking at the sight of two bodies locked together in a gesture of consolation as foreign and out of place.

I thought about how when Abuela caught us kids doing mischief, she would warn us with the phrase "Your abuelo's going to hit you." It was not "Your abuelo's going to get mad." The response to our wrongdoing went directly to the punitive.

When I became older, Tía Melania became open about how abusive Abuelo was to her and to Abuela. She had gotten involved with the church down the street from her house in Mexicali, where all González kids spent the summer. But I was the only one who was willing to accompany her to listen to the singing and praying. Perhaps because of this she was comfortable sharing a few details of the past.

"He made us walk around with handkerchiefs covering our heads like we were Muslim women or something," she said. We were walking along the dirt path. "He'd yank at my hair if he caught me outside without it. He was controlling and full of disdain."

"Is that why you ran away at fifteen?" I asked, familiar with the story of how she eloped quite young, which is why three of her children were older than me even though my father was the oldest sibling.

"I had to get away," she said. "Anything was better than living like that."

"Then why were we all living together in that apartment? Why didn't anyone say anything about Abuelo beating us?"

"Because that was nothing compared to how he treated us when we were young," she said. "Those González men, they are violent and terrible with their wives and children. I had a cousin whose face was broken by her father."

I found comfort in knowing that I had never seen my father lay a hand on my mother. I couldn't say the same for the other men.

"Weren't you afraid that he would come looking for you?" I asked. We arrived at the church gates. The sun was nearly setting and the light emanating from the entrance became brighter. Congregants gathered in the courtyard to exchange pleasantries and engage in small talk before the service.

"Oh, your father and uncle were mad at me for many years. Even your abuela."

"Why is that?"

"Because somebody had to pay the price of my escape."

I didn't need her to explain because I knew exactly what she meant.

"You know," she added as an afterthought, "you grandmother once left your grandfather."

Tía Melania didn't look back at me. She was revealing information that I wasn't entitled to. By staring straight ahead, it made it seem like less of an indiscretion. Besides, we were walking on sacred ground.

"When she found out about his affair with her cousin, the one they called La Tonche."

Of course, Abuelo cheated on Abuela. Why would he be different than many of the other González men?

"When your grandmother found out about La Tonche's pregnancy, she packed up her bags and walked out on him. The whole thing unfolded right there in my house while they were visiting. Your father had to drive down from California to help me deal with it. Personally, I was thrilled for my mother. Finally, she had rid herself of this man."

"Then, what happened?"

Tía Melania shook her head. "Well," she said solemnly, "the same thing that happens in many marriages like theirs. She didn't think she could raise your Tío Ramón on her own, and women just didn't leave their husbands like that in those days. Your father and I were discussing ways we could support your grandmother when all of a sudden here come your grandparents walking up the driveway like a pair of newlyweds, your grandfather carrying her suitcase in his hand."

Not much changed after that, except that Abuelo agreed never to talk to La Tonche or to seek out that child, a promise he kept until the child became an adult and visited Abuelo once or twice, introducing him to her family. During these short visits, Abuela hid herself in my father's house. I imagined how different Abuela's life would have been had she been able to remain separated, and how different all our lives would have been without Abuelo in our homes, let alone our lives. But that's not how it worked, and every decision made before I was born led to this moment: Tía Melania and me, chatting casually about our dysfunctional family that kept itself intact though it was quite broken.

We entered the church. Tía Melania always preferred the pews near the front. In order to romanticize the reason for this, I asked her once if she preferred sitting near the altar because she felt closer to God. And she responded, dead-pan, "No. I just want to be close to the heater."

She was practical. And so was my father and my uncles and my grandparents. When they agreed to share housing in California for a few years, it was because each immigrant family was too poor to live on its own. And since they had moved back in with Abuelo, the old dynamics took hold. That was the cost.

After that morning with Tío Ramón comforting Abuela at breakfast, I resolved to listen carefully to the sounds at night. When the TV and lights went out, I tried to remain awake and aware. It was easy to hear things from where I was sleeping, which was a large blanket on the floor I shared with my brother and the rest of our cousins. The linoleum floors did not squeak, but some people had heavier footfalls then others. I learned to distinguish them after a while. Sometimes I would forget about my nightly mission and surrender to sleep like everyone else, regretting my failure when I woke up the next day. But sometimes I did manage to stay awake, and the sounds of the apartment after dark surprised me.

The scratching in the kitchen, I knew, was a mouse. Tía Marta was committed to catching it because it ate through the boxes of her cake mix. She was charged with making the birthday cakes and she took the job seriously, becoming protective of her ingredients. She moved the mousetrap from one corner to the next. One night the mousetrap was triggered, and Tía Marta sprinted out of her room to check. If her footsteps didn't wake my cousins, the kitchen light did. The excitement was followed by an anticlimactic statement: "Damn trap. Nothing."

The cracking noises were made by the building structure itself, which was composed of five adjacent housing units held up by cement blocks. That's why the apartment had stairs at both entrances. No one was allowed to crawl underneath, even to retrieve a ball, because it was full of black widows, rats, maybe even snakes. Or maybe the whole thing might collapse and crush whoever dared wander under it. Every once in a while, I heard a crack, like firewood splitting in the flames.

"It's the house adjusting itself," my father said. "The weight of our bodies moves around all day. It's just trying to get comfortable again."

Crack! And I imagined its bones shifting back into place.

The old refrigerator sang all night. It was a sound drowned out during the daytime, but when everything quieted down, the humming and squeaking became amplified. The refrigerator seemed too small for such a large group of inhabitants, nineteen in all. And yet we all got fed. Just barely, but we managed it. If I walked past the kitchen to use the restroom at the end of the hall, the appliance seemed to glow in the dark. White and ghostlike, it huddled in its niche, chanting to itself to pass the time because it was our night watchman keeping vigil until breakfast.

And then there was a sound I couldn't locate in any particular room. It was a faint crying that squeezed itself between the cracking and humming so that it was almost inaudible. By its pitch I recognized it as a woman's cry. There were four possibilities: my mother, Tía Melania, Tía Marta, or Abuela. It was a cry that sounded lost, like the shrill of a wounded rabbit that came from the desert brush behind the building. The sound of distress was also its undoing because predators would be drawn to it. When the rabbit finally went quiet, it was because it had died or been killed.

For a day or two I became convinced that maybe this was a restless spirit, like the ones I had seen on TV with that ghost girl coming back to reclaim its doll. When the young kids found it for her, they laid it across her grave so that the spirit could finally rest in peace. I tried to convince my cousins, but they simply mocked me for believing such nonsense.

I decided to keep it to myself after that, a sacred knowledge about the place we inhabited that no one else knew or cared about—a communication from the great beyond that made this overcrowded apartment something special to boast about.

"My house is haunted," I would tell my friends at school, those who, like me, also trafficked in fantasy narratives like alien visitations. And they didn't need proof. Instead, they would shudder and then offer their own tales of hauntings at their homes.

When I felt like listening to the spirit, I waited patiently for the last TV program being watched to end, which cleared the air of all noise. I concentrated. There it was again, that crying, that spirit that was tearful over something or someone. Might there be a way to ask without alerting the rest of the household? Might I creep barefoot throughout the apartment looking for the source? Perhaps it was hovering in a ceiling corner with the spiderwebs or above a curtain, hiding in the blank space between the cloth and the metal rod. I imagined a small blue light, like the ghost girl's in that TV movie. Or maybe it was more celestial, like a soft white or yellow—the color of angel wings, angel faces.

I was about to drift off into sleep, hoping to take with me this search into dream. Maybe that world could offer me an answer or at least a direction by way of a symbol or a clue. There was a dream book for sale at Limon's Food Market. I came across it when I felt like leafing through the modest magazine stand. How I coveted the search word puzzle book, drawn to it after finding pleasure in the ones printed on cereal boxes. The dream book, with its strange illustration on the cover, hadn't called to me in a while, but this time it might prove useful.

I was about to doze off, quite satisfied with my plan, when suddenly I heard that second sound borne in close proximity to the crying. It was a *shhh*, so commanding and imposing that it silenced the cry immediately. And then there was silence. Even the hum of the refrigerator appeared to go dead.

That *shhh*, so human and brutish, dispelled the possibility of a ghost girl, shattering my hopes for an otherworldly encounter. That was a man's *shhh* muzzling the cries of a woman. Though this revelation did not bring me closer to identifying which husband and wife were having this conflict in the early hours. That's when my body began to shudder at the horrible truth of this mystery. If I couldn't pinpoint the culprits, that's because any married couple could be held responsible, even my own mother and father. No one was spared the suspicion of guilt.

It was like Tía Melania sparing no one when the window facing the empty back lot was broken. Any one of us kids was capable and therefore we were all penalized for an act that maybe one or two of us had committed. No use naming or blaming because she was sure to get it right by whacking all of us kids with a piece of the water hose. So too with the adults living under this roof: no use narrowing down which man was doing the beating or the hushing because any one of them had it in him, and any one of our mothers had to endure the violence.

I lay there, snug between other bodies as they breathed in and out, unaware of what was transpiring in the night. And because that woman, maybe my mother, or one of my aunts, or Abuela, had been banished into the void, I picked up where she left off and started whimpering.

Vanity

To say puerco: kuchi. As in Porky Pig.

—Abuela's lessons in Purépecha

DURING MY ADOLESCENCE, while living in El Campo with my grandparents, I recognized how uncomfortable they were with growing old. The black toothbrush in the medicine cabinet made sense finally after Abuelo walked out of the bathroom with a fresh coat of dye over his bristly mustache and eyebrows. Abuela laughed and I laughed with her, which didn't faze Abuelo one bit, even though his pitch-black hair looked strange, as if glued onto the worn skin around his face.

I had not seen gray on either of my grandparents. Both of them dyed their hair. It wasn't until their last years of life that my relatives commented on how differently they both looked with white hair. I didn't get to see that because I was living in New York City by then, with little desire to visit my relatives in California. I did visit my maternal grandparents in Michoacán and noted that they, on the other hand, embraced their aging with a sense of accomplishment, and they mentioned it often as a justification for why their grown children had to take care of them for a change.

"I'm old," Abuela Herminia would say to them with conviction. "It's your turn to feed me."

Abuela María refused to succumb to that mentality, and worked in the fields way past her retirement, which she did so willingly because she detested staying at home. Home was boring: a big TV in a cramped apartment, Abuelo in and out of midday naps, and two teenage grandsons who withdrew into their own interests—video games and books, respectively.

The boxes of hair dye were out in the open, but as a teenager I didn't understand what the big deal was. They were grandparents; they were supposed to look old. Both of them had loose skin under their arms, sunburned chests with a dull reddish-brown that appeared to be smeared on, and potbellies. Abuela, however, was much more attentive to her skin. After showering, she sat on the couch spreading a thick coat of cream over her face and hands that made her glow with the light of the TV. She didn't wear perfume, but the cream smelled flowery. She filled the living room with her scent.

The earliest memory I have of Abuela's vanity was a moment back in Michoacán when my grandparents were trying to convince my father to move his entire family to California. But since my mother was undocumented and her children were American citizens, we would have to be separated temporarily, Alex and I crossing the border before our parents. Abuela's job was to soften the blow of the plan to my brother and me. We cuddled next to her in bed one evening as she regaled us with stories about how schools fed us a delicious lunch every day and how we would learn English and be able to become supervisors at the agricultural fields. And Disneyland was in California too!

My mind spun with whimsical scenarios all evening. Finally, I would inhabit those kitchens and bedrooms that we saw every night in the American TV shows dubbed in Spanish. The couch always looked plush and inviting. A counter displayed sugar bowls and condiments, and people gathered around them to have serious conversations about family and school. And there were stairs inside the house. The concrete steps I was more familiar with led to the roof, where my mother would hang the clothes out to dry, and where I went to feed the dogs that barked at any passerby. Yes, I could have the couch and the kitchen. That was my destiny. Being an American made me special. Being in America even more so. That's what Abuela said.

On the evening when the final decision had been made, our family sat around the table eating tamales and atole, typical treats for the Christmas season. Tío Rafa and his wife, whose daughter, Verónica, was not an American citizen, were present too. After a lull in the conversation, my aunt burst out laughing.

"Can you believe that my mother-in-law smothers all that cream on her face to hide her wrinkles!" Tía Marta spurted out.

The silence that followed was uncomfortable. In hindsight, I recognized this cheap jab at Abuela's vanity as my aunt's resentment or even anger that an opportunity had been extended to one son and not the other, her husband. I don't recall this insult being addressed at the table. It might have been dealt with afterward, behind closed doors, but I do remember seeing Abuela look down at her food quietly as I wondered if those creams were why she looked moisturized, her dark skin glistening with the weak light of the dining room that made everyone else's faces appear sallow and dry.

Once we had moved to California, I didn't notice Abuela's beauty routine until the day she came out of the house to sit on the swing that hung from the old tree next to the schoolyard. My brother and I were playing baseball with a group of neighborhood kids using a tennis ball and a plank.

When Abuela approached, a peach in her hand, she sat without saying a word, but the other kids noticed her.

"Is that your mom?" one of them asked. Since my brother and I were the only Mexicans in the game, of course they would assume we were related to this Mexican lady.

"No," I said. "That's my grandma."

"She's pretty," someone else said.

In that moment I realized two things about Abuela. First, that she *was* pretty. Beautiful, in fact. Despite laboring in the fields and coming home each afternoon with a dusty bandanna around her head, she was quite feminine. She kept a basket of costume jewelry that she sifted through on the weekends, picking out the right pair of earrings to match her outfit. A pair of glass spheres hung from her earlobes that day, acting as prisms in the light. They complemented the crisp white blouse I had not noticed before.

She never wore anything but pants, however. And her hair was always cut short and combed back, which made her appear more masculine in her work clothes. But cleaned up and freshly moisturized with the large blue can of Nivea that took up space on the small bathroom counter, she was lovely to look at. Watching her slowly eating a peach was rather sensual.

The second thing I understood about her appearance that day was that it was intentional. She *wanted* to be seen because she knew she looked pretty. Enough to be mistaken for a younger woman. She may not have heard the flattery she was receiving from my friends, but she must have understood that she was being appreciated. I would learn about those admiring looks from strangers later in life.

During my childhood, however, I didn't think of myself as attractive, not with the excess weight that softened the features of my face. Abuela Herminia would call me handsome, but she said that about every man in her life. Besides, my aunts were quick to point out that my brother, Alex, was even more handsome. Abuela María, on the other hand, didn't pay me any compliments, not for my diligence in school or for my looks.

The only time I heard the adults mentioning my appearance took place while I was sitting on the couch, reading quietly. I was out of view from the gathering, which consisted of my parents, Tío Rafa and Tía Marta, Tía Melania, and Abuela.

Somehow the topic of looks came up, and they decided to single out the older group of cousins because we were all experiencing puberty and our bodies were changing. They spoke candidly, under the impression that none of us was in the house to overhear since there was no sound other than their chatter.

"Oh, she's going to be quite pretty," one of them said about my cousin Mari.

"He's going to be muscular and masculine," another said about my cousin Juve.

I wasn't paying much attention to the conversation, lost in the landscape of my book. But when I heard my name mentioned, I perked up.

"Rigo?" said my father. "Well, he's going to do well in school."

When the rest of the adults agreed, using guttural sounds, my face flushed. I snuck out of the living room to avoid notice and exited through the back door. I was well aware I hadn't inherited my father's good looks, but up until that moment I didn't realize that others had thought about it. Being good at school was such condescending praise. It was like receiving a participation ribbon at the school's art contest after the blue, red, and white ones were meted out—a pat on the head just for trying.

After my mother passed away, I would be told how much I resembled her. I always thought of my mother as beautiful, but when I looked in the mirror, I didn't see her. I saw a plump orphan with terrible wavy hair and crooked teeth. The baby fat was grotesque, as if my face was clinging on to childhood while my body grew larger and larger inside my clothes. I began to suspect that my relatives, especially those in Michoacán, wanted to maintain a connection to the woman who had just died by imposing this resemblance on me. Now I wasn't simply the least handsome of the two brothers; now I was the one who was keeping his mother's features alive. This was a pressure I didn't care for. I began to look for myself in that face, but that was made impossible when I stood next to my older cousins who were blossoming into thin bodies with the angles and curves that people appreciated in young men and women.

When I arrived with my older cousins at parties across the border, I sensed I was being looked at with pity.

"Oh, he's visiting," my cousins would say, explaining my presence. And the gathering of good-looking young people nodded knowingly. They too had an ugly duckling relative who was forced upon them once in a while.

I didn't think much about Abuela's appearance unless it was clearly a topic of conversation. Like the time her youngest son protested her wasting money on beauty products sold on TV.

"It's a scam, Amá," Tío Ramón said to her as he waved a carton box he had found hidden behind the sofa. On the box: the well-known logo for beauty products sold by Samy the celebrity Cuban stylist.

I was in middle school then, shocked that she was being confronted that way. I sat on the kitchen table doing my homework, slightly embarrassed for her. I was reminded of that incident with Tía Marta in Michoacán.

"These creams don't work, anyway. Do you see any difference?"

Abuela simply looked past her son and remained motionless. Since I was now older and I understood a moment of cruelty when I witnessed it, I yelled at my uncle in English.

"Leave her alone!" I said.

"Stay out of it," he said, side-eyeing me. "I'm trying to protect her from getting ripped off."

"It's her money," I added.

"And she's making a fool of herself. She's getting old and she can't do anything about it."

I sensed my grandmother's mortification at being reprimanded by her own son for taking care of herself. Only the single women in the family wore makeup. After marriage that habit faded because it was an unnecessary expense. Whatever beauty products were still around were brought out for special occasions, like weddings. Otherwise, such behavior was looked down upon, particularly by my aunts, who viewed it as frivolous and undignified.

Since we lived in a household of men, Abuela had no one to confide in about her need for these creams that promised to reawaken her youth. I wasn't sure why she would want that in the first place unless she was longing for something she had missed out on because she had married quite young. She was nineteen when my father was born. The same age that my mother was when I was born.

A photograph of Abuela's younger self sat on a display shelf, near the telephone. If anyone ever had occasion to make or answer a call, there was no choice but to gawk at the photograph of Abuela in her signature short hair, except that her skin was smooth and radiant.

It never occurred to me to imagine my grandmother as a younger woman, or even to ask about it. The closest we ever got to such a conversation was the time she was awkwardly trying to warn my brother and me about adolescent girls.

"You have to be careful with them," she said. "They can cause trouble."

She didn't have to say what kind of trouble. We were seeing for ourselves by way of our older cousins eloping with their girlfriends or coming home drunk after they got dumped. The pain of a breakup was a communal affair, with all of us cousins gathered around the devastated lover, offering words of consolation and encouragement. The adults stayed inside their rooms, allowing this ritual to take place undisturbed.

But when one of our cousins eloped, the adults took over, decrying the travesty, publicly disowning the stupid boy as a warning to the rest of us. The cousins would huddle in one of the rooms, the older ones pointing out the hypocrisy since most of our parents had done the same thing when they were young. "Even Abuela," one of them said.

I couldn't picture it. I couldn't see Abuela breaking such a rule. She was a good person. Every other adult was flawed in one way or another, but Abuela—she was a saint in my eyes. So, when she was trying to impart her wisdom about girls, and Abuela said, "When I was your age," my brain froze.

Of course, Abuela was my age once. But to me she was always Abuela María, the tiny older woman who looked after us. Was this a failing of how I had romanticized her matronly goodness? But such a projection also robbed her of her youth, of the life she had when she was younger. I must have done this with my grandfather also, except I had a contrasting opinion of him: to me he would always be the authoritarian, surly and mean. But he too was young once. I had seen those photographs as well. That masculine handsome man, however, had withered into this sun-burned balding middle-aged grandfather who struggled with high blood pressure and diabetes. No one shamed him for becoming an old man quite like his brother Tío Justo.

When Tío Justo arrived, he walked in and took over. He cooked and cut our hair—the two things Abuelo did best—and he sat on the couch criticizing whatever caught his attention.

"That clock isn't very impressive," he said, pointing with his chin. "I can get you a much better one and probably for less than what you paid for that one."

Abuela fumed a few feet away.

Tío Justo got up in the mornings and did his exercises in the yard. He brought his own hand grips and resistance bands. And although his training was evident in his pronounced biceps, which he showed off by rolling up his shirt sleeves, he was still a middle-aged man, not much younger than Abuelo. Yet he did have an energy that widened the gap between their ages.

The big difference between them was that Tío Justo was a bona fide sexist, making comments about women to the point that he became annoying even to the other men. My cousins simply dismissed him as an old pervert, and even my father, who could find humor in anything, sighed with exasperation when he couldn't keep the conversation focused.

"Whatever happened to that friend of yours, the one from Zacatecas?" Tío Justo inquired.

"Carmelo? Oh, you know him. Always busy with his daughters."

"Are they pretty? How old are they now?"

My father tried to move away from that line of thinking. "He's working for a construction company in Palm Desert."

"Lots of pretty women in Palm Desert," Tío Justo added.

I found it odd that Abuelo wouldn't challenge his younger brother's insults or that his younger brother didn't seem to have the same level of respect that his older brother had for him. Tío Justo wasn't more successful in life. He wasn't more handsome, or even thinner. If anything, Tío Justo made Abuelo look like a better person. I surmised that it must have been his brother's charisma and bravado that Abuelo admired—two characteristics that Abuelo lacked.

Since he was always on the go, Tío Justo's visits were brief, to everyone's relief, but he left quite an impression, particularly on Abuelo, who once bought a pair of hand grips, which he used for less than a week before giving them to my brother. Abuelo's enthusiasm for getting fit would lay dormant until Tío Justo's next visit.

I left home at seventeen. I didn't keep track of my grandparents' aging bodies. The more they aged the more like themselves they looked, meaning that I didn't expect to find anything other than a pair of old people becoming even older. They continued dyeing their hair, however.

My father displayed none of the anxieties his parents had. Like my mother's parents, he reveled in growing older, adopting a hat and a cane, which aged him even more.

"It's like a costume," my brother had noted.

When he lost a tooth, he wasn't self-conscious about it, and smiled big and wide like he always did. At this point, the effects of Parkinson's disease were wearing on him, but he didn't complain like Abuelo used to about his plight with blood sugar levels.

On a visit to Mexicali, I saw my father walking slowly past my brother's house, one of his daughters by his side.

"That shirt he's wearing makes him look homeless," I said. "Why doesn't his new wife clean him up? Why don't you buy him a shirt, for Christ's sake?"

"Dude," Alex said. "He likes to walk around like that. I've heard Amelia yell at him for insisting on wearing those raggedy shirts. He doesn't give a fuck what anyone says or thinks."

As I grew older, I realized that I would not take after my father but after Abuelo and Abuela. Seeing my body change, slow down, wear down, scar, stretchmark, and gray taught me that I wasn't ready to enter middle age. But that awareness about my body happened in phases. I had an opportunity to reinvent myself because I tore away from the family. Had I stayed, I would have remained the awkward book nerd with glasses and very little social skills.

I had always been a chunky child, a condition that made me vulnerable to teasing, not only at school but at home. That, combined with my effeminate nature, forced me to the margins of young male culture, and an outsider among the mostly male González household. That meant becoming the schoolboy who hid inside the library during recess and lunch from sixth to twelfth grade, avoiding all the rough and tumble antics of my gender. At home, I always had the perfect excuse—homework, and the fact that I was a voracious reader, a private and quiet activity my family seemed to encourage because they let me collect enough books to fill a shelf. Yet I always suspected this was because that made me one less troublemaker to deal with. All this focus on school and books made my imagination and intelligence blossom. I began to see the possibilities of an education—it could provide me with a life outside the agricultural fields and apart from this family that I was afraid would reject me anyway for being gay.

Without my brother or male cousins for camaraderie, I turned to my female cousins. The younger was a tomboy. She preferred the company of the other guys. But my cousin Mari, usually somber and secretive, welcomed me as her confidante, though I knew that she had many more things to say than what she offered me. Since she too was an outsider, we became de facto companions in California and in her childhood home in Mexicali while our parents were away, laboring in the hot agricultural fields in the summer.

Mari and I remained close until I told her I was moving away to college. We went together to the Goodwill thrift store. Her boyfriend at the time agreed to drive us there and drop us off.

"What kind of clothes do college boys wear?" she asked as soon as we started to sift through the bins. Mari, like her two brothers, had dropped out of school in her teens, unable to adapt to American education after their household migrated. Our purpose that day was to make me more presentable for a journey no one before me had made.

I thought back on the films with college settings. Images of young white men in sweaters with insignias popped into my head, the crisp collars of their dress shirts poking out, crisp as folded paper. We couldn't find any such sweaters there, but we did find a few sweater vests. They looked drab and out-of-style, but college was an entirely different world. Certainly, they had their own unique dress.

Needless to say, I discarded those sweater vests not long after I moved into the dorms. Not only was no one wearing sweaters and dress shirts, but many walked around very relaxed and unpreoccupied about what they wore—pajama bottoms, flip-flops, raggedy shirts that even Goodwill wouldn't resell—so I concluded that my jeans and short-sleeved cotton shirts would work out just fine.

I was still slightly overweight when I started college. But unlike high school, there wasn't much shaming about clothing or body size—at least nothing I was aware of. Like the other college kids who only months before were high school seniors, I recognized that I had graduated to another level of social interaction, particularly in the dorms, where much of our meal conversation centered around our classes, our test grades, and our homesickness.

During this time, however, I was tricked into starting to exercise. Gym was one of my anxieties in high school. I was afraid of male bodies as much as I was attracted to them. But with my excess weight and short height, I felt especially inferior to the lean and athletic young men who moved about the locker rooms with such confidence. I was relieved to find out that in college, any extracurricular activity was optional.

Since I had grown up connected to my cousin Mari, it was natural for me to establish friendships with the young women in the dorms who embraced me as a brother. And as the brother, I was enlisted to escort many of them from their labs or evening classes to the dorms. Eventually, they also had me tag along on late-night visits to the mall, movie theaters, or Denny's, the college hangout. I made them feel safe. And though I wasn't out to any of them at this point, I sensed they knew—why else would they restrain from all flirtation and ask me for my opinions about their appearance before they went out on dates with other college guys?

Most of these young women were first-generation college students like me, all of us children of immigrants from México, Vietnam, China, Japan, and India. On one occasion, my friend Thuy asked me to accompany her to the Health Center on campus. I didn't think anything of it, particularly because Thuy had a thick accent that took some getting used to. She didn't tell me why she needed to go to the Health Center, and I didn't ask any questions. We entered the crowded lobby and walked up to the reception counter.

Thuy looked at me, which I understood was my cue to speak on her behalf.

"She needs to see a doctor," I said.

"Are you here together?" the receptionist asked.

"Yes," I said naively. That seemed like an obvious response. We handed her our student IDs.

She gave us two separate clipboards and we signed in with our personal information, taking a seat in the lobby with the rest of the college kids.

Our wait wasn't long, despite the number of bodies in the lobby. We were called up, but to my surprise, Thuy and I were separated. This was my first time at the Health Center. I didn't want to question their procedures. I was led to a room where an older woman greeted me kindly.

"How are you doing?" she said. I gave one-word answers, uncertain about what was unfolding before me.

"Well, let's talk about venereal diseases," she said.

I became so nervous that I broke into a sweat. What had Thuy gotten me into? I sat patiently through the whole speech about different types of diseases that college students were susceptible to. She spoke about symptoms and treatments. Blood was drawn, along with a gentle prod to exercise more because my blood pressure was too high. And we ended the session with a promise to come back for a battery of tests. "It all depends on your blood test results and that of your girlfriend's," she said.

After I met with Thuy back in the lobby, I didn't know what to say. We walked back to the dorms without saying a word to each other, or to anyone else.

On another occasion, it was my friend Elsa from Tijuana who got me embroiled in another situation, but one that led to a decade-long relationship with dance. She was the most Mexican of Mexicans. That's what we other Mexicans said about her. For many of us, there was a bit of shyness in expressing ethnic pride. We had yet to shake off that "fitting in" pressure we caved to in high school. We first saw Elsa as she walked into the dorm cafeteria with her big smile and loud voice. As she looked around the room, the food tray in her hands, I had the inkling that she was going to spot our cluster.

"Hey, are you guys Mexican?" she asked.

"Well, some of us," said one of my friends.

"Okay!" Elsa squeezed her tray on the table. "I'm Elsa. I'm from Tijuana."

Elsa earned her Mexican of Mexicans designation by heating up menudo on Sundays and making buñuelos for people's birthdays. We would walk around with these huge deep-fried treats on our hands as the white kids marveled at the "giant cookies." She also played Los Bukis tapes when she cleaned her room, the door wide open for the entire hall to hear. She was a science major, but she had a passion for ballet folklórico, the traditional Mexican dances that varied in dress, music, and steps, according to each Mexican state or region.

In my role as safety escort, I met her outside the science building as usual, but she came down with a pair of white shoes with thick heels and a colorful skirt.

"I have a favor to ask," she said. "Can you walk me to the theater?"

I followed this routine for weeks. Partly because this was one more connection to our homeland. Folk dance was a joyful expression of cultural pride. The skirt movements changed with each new region: Jalisco was aggressive; Veracruz was gentler; Michoacán, my home state, had a stronger Indigenous influence and therefore the women hiked up the skirt daintily

with their fingertips, only enough to show the footwork, which they performed in sandals or barefoot. The music transported me to the crowded
cultural festivities in México, where my favorite street vendor treat was a
pancake topped with caramel.

"If only we had a guy," the dance instructor said.

It didn't occur to me before, but this dance troupe only had female
dancers.

As if on cue, they all turned to look at me from the stage.

At first, I resisted. I didn't know how to dance. I never went to a single
dance without my cousins to hide behind.

"Come on, Rigo, come on," Elsa pleaded.

I climbed onto the stage and stayed there, connecting to a Mexican
dance troupe at every city I moved to for the next ten years.

The long rehearsals, particularly during Cinco de Mayo season, kept me
active and fit. The shift to dorm food—a far cry from the fatty, starchy
meals I had at home—also contributed to my incredible weight loss, which
alarmed my grandparents whenever I visited. In the first few years of my
life as a dancer, I shed seventy pounds.

During performances, if I was the only male dancer, I would have to share
the dressing room with all the female dancers. A nonthreatening presence,
I wasn't shy about taking off my pants in front of them and neither were they
embarrassed to be seen in bras and bloomers. There was hardly time to
think about such things between costume changes among the chaos of shoes,
skirts, and fake braids. But my body transformation did not go unnoticed.

"Rigoberto's looking fine, isn't he?" I heard one of them say. "That nice
ass on him."

Once I admired what I saw in the mirror—narrow waist, broad chest, and
muscular legs—I became determined to keep it that way. Suddenly I wasn't
that chubby friend of all women anymore, I was that handsome young dancer
who received plenty of attention from men and women. During my college
years, I slept with both.

Sex into my twenties was a liberating stage. I preferred homosexual encounters, though for one year I dated Vikki, a Taiwanese woman—an experience I kept from my gay friends because I feared any judgments. Bisexuals

were either deemed sluts because they would "sleep with anybody" or viewed negatively as homosexuals in denial. I didn't engage in any sexual identity politics. Whatever I did, with whomever, was my business. I adhered to that motto until my late thirties, which is when I began to succumb to a neurological illness the doctors never quite pinpointed, but whose effects severely compromised my movement and my appearance.

By the age of forty, I weighed 230 lbs. and maneuvered through New York City with the aid of a cane. My depression led to drinking, which led to my struggles with hypertension and swollen feet. The more I looked at myself, the more dejected I became that I had lost track of that fit young dancer who could bounce back quickly after each exhausting performance on stage.

During this period in my life, I kept myself hidden from my family and friends. I refused to visit or even be seen, pouring my energy into my writing, which also gave me the excuse to turn down invitations to social events.

The moment of reckoning came when the doctor predicted that if I continued on this downfall, I would need the aid of a wheelchair. As a resident in New York City, I realized that this would be too much of an inconvenience, particularly because I commuted from Queens to New Jersey for work. My small studio apartment was claustrophobic already, and the thought of maneuvering a wheelchair into an ill-equipped space filled me with dread. This was not a tenable situation for me.

My brother, who had been going through a similar health decline, became my sole source of support. Together we convinced ourselves that we had to reverse course.

"We really have no excuse," I said to him during our weekly phone call. "We have access to information, we have resources. Our grandparents and our father suffered because they didn't know how to help themselves."

The body transformation took about five years, but we managed it. My brother lost thirty pounds and I lost fifty, which made a huge difference in our ability to move around but also in our appearance. Each week we reconnected, sharing our good news.

"My pants are loose again, Turrútut," Alex said. "I couldn't even keep them up with a belt."

"I'm down to a size thirty-three," I said. "I haven't been size thirty-three since I was in my early thirties!"

My doctors were pleased that I had avoided becoming diabetic like my grandfather and encouraged me to keep going, to start toning and building muscle. But now that I was aware of my body again at age forty-five, that vain gene kicked in. I pulled out from under the sink all the scrubs and face creams I had neglected during my illness. White hair had begun to sprout around my temples and the back of my head. But most alarming of all was the loose skin around my stomach, and my sunken face.

"I don't look forty-five, I look fifty-five," I complained to a friend.

We hadn't seen each other in years, and now that I felt presentable again, I wanted to show off my new look. We met for brunch in The Village, and he was impressed I had skipped the bottomless mimosas because he had known me back in the day when I was a heavy drinker.

"Well, you know there are things you can do about the way you look," he said.

"More creams? Hair dye? God, I don't want to become my grandparents."

My friend laughed. "You are a funny boy, aren't you? Listen, you're a grown-up now with no children and plenty of disposable income. Do what many of us middle-aged gays are doing: get work done."

The more pressing issue I wanted to address was the loose skin around the belly. I had become self-conscious about it during sex. Abdominoplasty, the plastic surgeon called it, because the phrase "tummy tuck" was a procedure connected to women. Soon after, I used Botox to erase the wrinkles and the fillers to bring back my cheeks and chin.

My other good friend Eduardo was not pleased.

"I knew it," he said. "As soon as you told me about the first surgery, I knew you weren't going to be able to stop. You're almost fifty! You think people aren't going to notice?"

I had a flashback of Tío Ramón reproaching Abuela about her Productos Samy.

"It's my money and my body," I said, which is exactly how I had wanted Abuela to answer back.

"Well, just don't overdo it," he warned. "You're going to become one of those ridiculous plastic queens who thinks everyone believes he's under forty."

I continued my visits to my plastic surgeon for the next five years, maintaining a wrinkle-free face while observing that those who were aging naturally were leaving me behind. Some commented on my smooth skin, asking for my beauty secrets. Sometimes I would be honest and let them know that I was getting work done, and other times I lied through my teeth like the celebrities on talk shows who declared that the most important steps to staying young were getting enough sleep, drinking plenty of water, and staying out of the sun.

"No one buys that," Eduardo said to me.

To explain away my new practice as simple vanity didn't capture the complex relationship I had with my appearance. My ugly duckling adolescence, my late blossoming in college, my collapse in my thirties, and my rebirth in my forties told a more complicated story. The next phase was just as thorny: I was entering my grandparents' age when they were partnered in a fervent dedication to preserving their youth.

In Purépecha, the word for skin is sïkuiri, but the word for animal hide is pasïri. I don't know if Purépechas apply the words the way Mexicans did when they distinguished piel from pellejo. Piel is youthful skin, desirable and appealing. That picture of Abuela next to the telephone was taken with a filter I have seen used in those portrait studios that make dark people look lighter, older people look younger, and plain faces appear better-looking— presentable, eliciting compliments. Keep your mouth closed to hide your imperfect teeth. How handsome. How pretty. No, not the person standing on two feet in the living room but their image in that picture. The camera can lie.

Pellejo was old skin. Worn skin. What hardened on a carcass. What became obscene with flies buzzing about and hairs exposed in the light. Decaying pork rind. Pellejo was improper and unseemly. It contracted, crushing muscle and bone, making the body shrink. A smaller, less socially acceptable version of the self now roamed the room, the streets. You didn't

turn heads anymore. You were a thing relegated to the sidelines, uninterest-
ing and negligible. If it was worth looking at, it was because it was worth
ridiculing.

"How is your father doing?" a woman at the market asked another woman.

Abuela and I were standing behind them, waiting our turn to pay for
groceries.

The second woman waved her arm dismissively and said, "Ya es puro
pellejo." He's all skin, all waste.

Abuela turned to me and let out that naughty giggle she offered whenever she overheard an insult that she found amusing. Abuela never called
herself old, though she called other people that, especially those she found
objectionable. She hurled that word—old—to mean worthless, useless,
clumsy, and stupid. She didn't see herself as any of those things. But it was
getting more and more difficult to deny that she was aging.

Decades of over-the-counter dye had damaged her hair. In the last years
of her life, it looked dry and coarse. She had given up trying to keep it pitch-
black and started applying a browning tint to her hair that made it look the
color of roadkill.

She had discontinued purchasing creams once she became a widow because
of her fixed income. And it never occurred to me to supply them for her,
though I should have. I was buying them for myself. Instead, Abuela resorted
to other measures, like growing a maguey plant. Akamba, she called it, in
her tongue.

"What's Abuela trying to do?" I once asked my brother as I watched her
tend to her plants. "Is she going to harvest her own tequila now?"

My brother and my sister-in-law, Lupe, looked over with disinterest. This
was yet another visit in which I had to observe from afar because Abuela no
longer accepted visitors. Not even me.

"She wants sábila," Lupe said. "It's curative. For burns. But she also uses
it on her face when she runs out of baby oil. She's going to cook her skin
right off one day."

My sister-in-law had used the word pellejo, not piel.

People will ask me when I reveal that I'm frequenting a plastic surgeon, "Why do you do it?" That was not a question I ever posed to my

grandparents, but I suspect that, like me, they wouldn't have a satisfactory answer. Trying to fix the outside covered up the fact that the inside remained unaddressed. When people looked at me as I was growing up, I was afraid they saw only that doughy little boy with crooked teeth and feminine mannerisms. And later, I wanted to escape the image of an obese middle-aged man on a cane. Changing my appearance was one way to take back control, as irrational as that sounds. Was it the same for my grandparents? What did I see outside of an old cranky man in Abuelo? Or a soft-spoken old woman in Abuela? Perhaps they wanted to see themselves as more than that, and to demand that others adopt that vision.

Vanity might be easily identified, but it is impossible to explain. It had a hold on my grandparents, who were working-class farmworkers living in subsidized housing. And with the same claw it had taken possession of me, an upper-middle-class professional living in a doorman building in New York.

After retirement, Abuela and Abuelo moved to Mexicali, next door to my brother and his family. And after Abuelo passed away, Abuela only spoke to people through the fence. When she needed something, she would come out and call to my brother as soon as she saw him puttering around in his front yard.

"Beni," she called to him, using the childhood nickname she had given him.

"Yes, Abuela," my brother said.

"Don't you notice anything different about me?"

Abuela posed. Alex had been noting how she was becoming more confused with age, and he had raised the alarm a few times with Tía Melania, letting her know that Abuela wasn't taking good care of herself.

"No, I don't, Abuela," my brother said finally. "What is it?"

"You don't notice it?"

Alex let out a slight giggle. "No, I don't."

The other concern Alex had about Abuela was that she was losing her sight.

"I'm getting younger," she said. "I looked in the mirror this morning and I realized that my wrinkles have gone away."

Abuelo kept dying his hair until he was no longer capable. In the last year of his life, his white hair had grown out, rendering him nearly unrecognizable.

"He had bigger worries," Alex said as he described the last photograph of Abuelo in his wheelchair, parked underneath an orange tree.

"He tried to bite into an orange hanging from a branch," Alex said.

Since he could no longer swallow properly after his stroke, Abuelo had been placed on an all-liquid diet, which made him smaller. At his funeral, he was someone else altogether. Someone had made the decision to cut off his mustache, which had been his pride and joy all his life.

"There was a stranger in that coffin," Alex said.

Each year, as I see myself age and try to fight it with Botox and collagen injections, I can't help but imagine that Abuela, and maybe even Abuelo, would have done the same thing had they had the resources. There will come a time when I can no longer afford or make those decisions for myself, but until then I'll keep doing what I want, without anyone's permission or approval. Just like Abuela did in the last years of her independence.

"What are you going to do to yourself next?" my cynical friend asked.

"Who knows? Maybe a Brazilian butt lift," I responded.

Roadside Chat

Vaca is what here? Cow. Cow es uakasï.

—Abuela's lessons in Purépecha

WHILE ATTENDING COLLEGE at the University of California, Riverside, I dated a woman during my junior and senior years. I met Vikki through her roommate, who was a friend of mine. Since we all gathered at their apartment on the weekends to joke around and play stupid drinking games, Vikki and I developed a special friendship, particularly because we both loved Chinese food and shopping at the local mall. Vikki, daughter of a Taiwanese international real estate agent, had money to spend and I helped her spend it, giving her advice on which dress looked more flattering and what color lipstick worked well with her skin tone. We became close because there was no sexual tension between us: I was her gay friend. During those weekends when everyone slept over, too drunk to get home, it was me who was allowed to share a bed with Vikki. We shocked our friends when that friendship turned into intimacy.

"But aren't you gay?" Vikki's roommate said incredulously.

"I guess I'm bi," I said, and we left it at that. In college, the days went by too fast to slow down and truly examine such a thing, especially with our small group, which prided itself over its outsider status. We were not like the normies, we declared, though I'm certain many other cliques thought the same.

Vikki and I had an understanding. This was a college fling. Her parents would never allow her to marry a man who was not Taiwanese. They were so protective of her that when they caught wind of the weekend parties, they insisted Vikki kick the roommate out so that she could live alone for the rest of the year. That allowed me to spend most of my free time with her, sleeping over all week except when her parents came down from Rancho Palos Verdes to check in on her.

I made the mistake of introducing her to my grandparents one time because Vikki loved Mexican food and she wanted to try out the real thing. We drove down to El Campo for a home-cooked meal: pork in green sauce and Mexican rice.

From the moment we stepped in through the door, Abuela was dazzled. She chuckled because Vikki was even shorter than she was, and pretty in her tight-fitting dress. Both Vikki and Abuela had small feet, and that amused Abuela to no end as she constantly looked down at them during our visit. Abuelo was also pleased and immediately assumed we were going to get married.

"She won't be the first Asian in the family. Tell her that," he commanded. "Tell her about your Tía Yunko from Japan who married my brother Baltazar. Tell her they have a son who is half Japanese and half Mexican. Tell her he's a dentist. Such a smart boy."

I became exhausted translating back and forth, and slightly annoyed that Abuelo got on the phone and called over Tío Rafa and Tía Melania to come look at this petite Asian bride-to-be that I had brought home.

"She's not going to be the first Asian to marry into the family," Abuelo declared proudly to each person who arrived. "Remember Yunko?"

Vikki took it all in stride, unoffended that some of my younger cousins, who had likely not seen an Asian person this close, stared at her and even dared to inspect her as if she were a mannequin on display. My older cousins were ruthless, however.

"Are you going to teach her to make beans?" one said.

When I got up from the table to get her a second helping of pork and rice, they laughed.

"Look at this little thing. She's got Rigo trained already. Can we get you an apron, cousin?"

That was the first and only time I dared bring Vikki home, and eventually my family asked about her less and less, except for Abuela, who even asked for a picture of Vikki, which she framed and kept on her TV for many years while still inquiring about her: "And Vikki?"

By that point, years had passed since we ended our relationship. I found it heartwarming that Abuela held on to hope, as if one day I would surprise her with a different answer than my usual reply: "She's fine. She's back in Taiwan." I wouldn't learn about how invested Abuela had become in Vikki until a series of decisions conspired to strand Abuela and me in the dangerous canyons of Freeway 60, heading toward Riverside, where I lived during my undergraduate years. In that cheap Riverside apartment, I lived with a few roommates I rarely saw, one of them a white guy who was a friend of Vikki's and the other a Chinese exchange student who spent most of the day in the labs.

I had convinced my brother to join me on a train ride from Mexicali to Guadalajara, where we would then board a bus to Zacapu. Since it was the middle of summer, Pacific hurricane season was at its height. This was a momentous trip because I had opted to skip the exhausting two-day bus ride and take the much-talked-about passenger train of el Ferrocarril Nacional de México, which was trying to encourage more railway travel after the five regional railroads had merged into a single conglomerate in 1987. The freight service wasn't going well for them because of stiff competition from the trucking and shipping companies. Desperate, they touted their passenger cars as more comfortable and less dangerous than a bus. Not to mention faster.

"It's going to be an adventure," I told Alex. "And we'll get to Michoacán in no time! Don't you want to see Abuela Herminia and Abuelo Melecio?"

Alex knew it was only a ploy, that I had invited him because he had a car and therefore would be my ride to Mexicali. That was true, but also, I was nervous about making this journey alone. The only other time we traveled by train was after our mother's death in Michoacán. We couldn't afford airline tickets from Mexico City to Mexicali. The next best thing was the railroad, which turned out to be a disaster because the train broke down a few hours after boarding in Guadalajara. Abuela María, Tío Rafa, and our father were on this ill-fated trip, reassuring us through the night that everything would be fine.

"This train's a thousand times better than the crappy one we rode in back in the day," I told him, though I had no idea if that was true.

I hitched a ride to El Campo, where Alex still lived with Abuela María and Abuelo Ramón. I helped Alex pack his clothes in a duffle bag similar to mine.

"Less bulk, less hassle," I explained.

Abuela watched from the doorway while we were packing.

"And Vikki?" she asked.

"She's in Riverside," I said. "She's going to get picked up by her parents this week."

"You should have invited her to go to Michoacán with you," Abuela said. "To introduce her to your mother's parents. Tu témba." She grinned when she used the Purépecha word for wife.

"Some other occasion, Abuela," I said.

"Well, then maybe I can go with you," she said.

I looked at Alex. It hadn't occurred to me to ask Abuela if she wanted to come. I didn't think Abuelo would allow it. The visit was only going to last two weeks, but I couldn't imagine Abuelo letting Abuela out of his sight for that long.

"Well, if you want to come, pack your bags," I said. "What will Abuelo say?"

To our surprise, Abuelo thought it was a good idea. That way we could all be together and stay at his sister Sara's place. She had room.

I cringed. Alex and I had absolutely no plans to visit any of our relatives from Abuelo's side of the family. And I expected Abuela didn't either. Since all her siblings also lived in Zacapu, she had choices. But I knew that Abuelo's permission was precarious, so I agreed with his suggestion.

That night, I could hardly sleep. I began to fantasize about our arrival and the joy we were about to experience as Alex and I walked up the street to our grandparents' house. Abuela Herminia might be tending to her roses in the garden. Abuelo Melecio might be sitting on the sidewalk, eating peanuts and waving at the passersby. From the front entrance we could see the kitchen and one of our aunts—we wouldn't be able to tell which one because she would be all shadow with the light behind her coming from the indoor courtyard, but she would be at the stove, stirring a large tin serving spoon. Yes, we were hungry.

But just then, I froze. I had forgotten my American birth certificate, my only way back into the U.S. I jolted up and whispered into Alex's ear, waking him from sleep.

"Dude," I said. He looked at me annoyed. "Tomorrow before driving to Mexicali, we'll have to drive back to Riverside to pick up my birth certificate. I forgot it."

"Stupid," he said.

"Will you do that? I'm paying the gas."

"Okay!" he said, and then rolled over in bed.

His consent to make the extra trip gave me some peace of mind, but I still didn't sleep much that night.

The next day we had an early breakfast, said good-bye to Abuelo, and then headed out, though instead of going south, we went north. We decided not to tell Abuela until we were in the car. She didn't say anything, though I was certain she thought I was an idiot for leaving behind such an essential document.

The eight-mile journey was uneventful until we reached the canyons of Moreno Valley. The highway curved left and right, making it difficult to see what was coming up. A cement divider separated southbound traffic from northbound, but the two lanes on each side were narrow. The risk on the left lane was striking the divider; the risk on the right lane was plummeting down the ravines. I was confident in my brother, however, because he was an excellent driver. Vikki rarely let me drive her car because I became too nervous, especially on the freeway.

Alex's skills were put to the test when one of the back tires blew out. He maneuvered the car without swerving, and I thanked the stars I had not been behind the wheel because I would have panicked and killed us all. Alex stepped out to confirm the damage.

"Now what?" he said.

"Now I call Vikki."

In the era before cell phones, emergency call boxes were placed all along the road. I opened the yellow metal door and picked up the receiver. There was no way to dial, but the phone started ringing.

"How may I help you? Is this an emergency or do you need roadside assistance?" the voice said.

This is how it worked: I gave the operator a number to call if I had one, otherwise she would alert a towing company. After giving her Vikki's number, the operator asked me to stand by. A few minutes later, she informed me that Vikki had received directions to my location and would arrive shortly.

While Vikki made her way, Alex removed the tire.

"I'll just get it fixed at a nearby gas station," he said.

Abuela sat expressionless in the back seat. I had flashbacks of that time we were stranded on the train. When night fell, everything was pitch black because we broke down in a forest. The heat and humidity were unbearable, especially for the women who didn't dare exit the train to cool off the way the men had. I wanted to apologize to Abuela, but I decided to wait until we were back on the road again.

Somehow Vikki found us. She had to go past us to make a U-turn. When she finally pulled up behind us, I greeted her with a kiss.

"Sorry, Bird," I said, using the nickname I had given her after we became a couple.

"That's okay," she said.

Alex acted quickly. Vikki popped open the trunk, the damaged tire was thrown in, and off they went to get it repaired. I waited with Abuela in the car.

"That poor girl," Abuela said. "Driving out here in the middle of nowhere."

"I know, Abuela," I said. "What choice did I have?"

After a brief silence, perhaps taking pity on the guilt weighing me down, Abuela changed the subject.

"What are your intentions with that girl, anyway?" she asked. "Clearly she likes you. Are you going to ask her to marry you?"

How to explain to Abuela what a complicated relationship Vikki and I had? I had introduced Vikki to my ex-boyfriend at a party once and she didn't even flinch. She had once made out with her ex-roommate Olga over a game of spin-the-bottle. Anything went in college. I spared Abuela those details, but I did want to confide in her.

"Her parents don't want her to marry me," I said, which was the truth. They would only accept a Taiwanese groom.

"Why not?" she said. "You're going to be a teacher; you'll have a profession."

"It's not as easy as that," I said. Speeding cars zoomed by. The temperature was rising steadily. Abuela was starting to sweat.

"Don't you want to marry her?" she asked.

Vikki and I had agreed to part ways after college. I had plans to attend a graduate program in English literature at a university in northern California. She would most likely move back with her parents, eventually returning to Taiwan. Still, I had proposed to her the idea of getting hitched.

"Marry? What for?" she said earnestly.

"I don't know," I said awkwardly. "Maybe to have kids."

"Kids? No way! You go have kids. Not me."

Getting married and having kids seemed like the fastest way back to familiar territory. I had only been out of the closet for a few years, and thus far, I wasn't impressed with the men I encountered. Gay men in their twenties were interested in partying, going to the clubs, snorting meth, cruising. Like me, many of them had come from repressed environments and college was a time of unleashing, surrendering to urges, passions, and vices. Waking up in a stranger's bed was not something to worry about. Remembering where the car was parked was. "I'll catch you later" was the compulsory statement made as the one-night stand exited the apartment. And the following week at the club, the men might nod at each other because they had revealed their bodies to each other, but that was last week. This week was about seeking out the next encounter.

A boyfriend was a partner in crime, convenient until one tired of the other. There were plenty to choose from. College was fertile with potential mates.

A girlfriend, on the other hand, was singular. On a college campus, the hand-holding signaled monogamy, or whatever passed for commitment among the undergraduate population. Girls didn't get passed around without judgment or contempt. When I had a boyfriend, the relationship was private. When I had a girlfriend, it was public. How did I want to move in the world—in the shadows or in the light?

"I did tell her I wanted us to get married," I explained to Abuela. "But she has different plans."

Abuela went quiet for a few minutes. I thought that that would be the end of that conversation. I didn't expect her to speak up again. When she did, I was startled.

"There's only one way," she said.

"One way for what?"

"To make sure she marries you."

I had a funny feeling about where this was going. Elope, like many of our family members had done? Vikki would never go for that.

"Just take her," Abuela said.

I stared at her, confused. "Take her? What do you mean?"

"Impregnate her," Abuela answered, deadpan.

I couldn't hold back a chuckle. But when I realized she was serious about her suggestion, I felt a stone in my stomach. I didn't have time to process it further because Vikki and Alex returned. In a matter of minutes, Vikki drove off again as Alex changed the tire, and then we resumed our trip back to my apartment to retrieve my birth certificate. Less than half an hour later, we were southbound.

The excitement of the incident had exhausted us. We didn't speak much during that two-hour drive to the border. We made one stop for gas and another for food. When I handed Abuela her tray with a small burger and fries, we exchanged an awkward look that even Alex couldn't ignore.

"What's going on?" he asked. "Is she mad you dragged her all the way to Riverside?"

"Not that," I said. "I'll tell you later." But that moment didn't come until we were in our forties.

Once we arrived in Mexicali, we were met with the bad news that the trains had been canceled because the coastline had been pummeled by Hurricane Fefa and Hurricane Guillermo. The damage to the railroad tracks was not easily repaired. Alex, Abuela, and I made a vacation of it anyway, staying in Tía Melania's house, which was usually a flurry of activity because it was summer and her five children were around to wreak havoc and plan parties and gather the neighborhood kids for soccer matches in the back lot. Alex was in his element.

Tía Melania was pleased to spend time with her mother without Abuelo around. And she said as much any chance she got, though this was short-lived because Abuelo decided to drive down after finding out the trip to Michoacán was a bust.

As soon as he arrived, he took over the kitchen and the cookouts, ordering the women around like a manager. During mealtimes, Abuela would sit under a large eucalyptus tree that stood in the backyard, a plate on her lap. She looked at peace, regardless of the summer's outcome. I couldn't help but stare at her from a distance, wondering what complicated thinking was going on in her head.

"Impregnate her," she had said. By force? Seduction? Vikki and I had an active sex life, but we took precautions. I lived in a world different from Abuela's youth, when a pregnancy meant obligation, no matter how that child was conceived. My father was her firstborn. Was that why my grandparents had remained together all this time? Out of obligation and then out of habit? I looked at Abuelo, griping as usual, this time about the salsa because someone else had made it.

"Maruca!" he called to Abuela, holding out the bowl. "Go in and make a better one than this. This tastes like tomato juice."

Tía Melania narrowed her eyes in displeasure.

Abuela got up obediently and took the bowl, looking down at it with pity. She dipped her finger to taste it.

She looked back at Abuelo and said, "You're right, Perrillo. No bite at all." Tía Melania's body tensed. Her face remained frozen.

The story Tía Melania told me about Abuelo and Abuela's first meeting was this: Abuelo and Tío Justo, young men at the time, set out on a search for any job in their hometown of Zacapu, and walked into the local bakery, a tiny one owned by Papá Juan. Papá Juan took the eager young men under his tutelage, though it didn't take long for Ramón and María, the baker's oldest daughter, to start making eyes at each other.

"Papá Juan was such a wonderful baker," she said. "But that bakery was doomed. All his relatives came by with their huge baskets to stock up on bread. None of them paid a cent and Papá Juan was too kind to ask for money. Eventually, that bakery went bankrupt."

Tía Melania spoke tenderly about Papá Juan, but she rarely had anything positive to say about his descendants.

"Mamá Lola didn't like your grandfather," she continued. "She thought he was lazy and warned your grandmother not to get too close to him. Papá Juan didn't say a negative word about anyone. When your grandparents started dating, he didn't discourage it. I think he saw your grandfather as a potential heir to the bakery. But of course, that didn't work out. Very few things turn out the way one imagines them."

Did the life Abuela dreamed about look anything like this?

I took my plate of food and sat in Abuela's empty chair. I wanted to keep the seat warm. I wanted to make sure to save her favorite spot under the eucalyptus tree. From a safe distance, apart from the rest of the family, I felt sheltered and calm. A leaf dropped on my lap and I let it sit there, undisturbed, while Abuelo's barking drifted farther and farther away.

THIRD INTERLUDE

Class of '88

THE FIRST TIME I SPOKE OF AIDS was with a girl in my journalism club during our senior year in high school. Lisa and I were laying out the latest issue of *Sandscripts* before it got sent out to be typeset and printed. She was the master of photograph dimensions and knew how to adjust the size of a picture on the page to accommodate the text. I was the word counter, turning each article from paragraphs to column inches. As newshounds, we had to keep up with the goings on in the school and then reduce them to digestible snippets for our readers. My beat was academics. I got to interview the latest Student of the Month, the new vice principal, and the tournament champions of the Debate Club. The outside world didn't enter the halls through the newspaper but through the chatter between classes, or during lunchtime club activities, which is when Lisa casually mentioned the subject of AIDS.

"I wouldn't be afraid of a person who had it," she said. "Unless I had a cut or a sore on my finger. Then I wouldn't feel safe shaking hands."

I didn't want to point out how contradictory her statement sounded because at the time I wasn't confident about pushing back. I didn't want to ask her where she had gotten her information from because clearly this was common knowledge. Once again, I felt embarrassed that I lived in a Mexican household in which the news came to us in Spanish, where the elegant anchors mentioned SIDA by name once in a while but not much else. It was all a big mystery.

"How can you tell if someone has AIDS?" I asked.

Lisa looked at me in disbelief. "Well, if a person is gay or a drug addict, they're likely to have AIDS," she said with certainty.

I nodded my head, though I didn't see the connection between the two. Except that in our community these were the outcasts and undesirables who lurked the neighborhood after dark. "Don't go out at night," warned Abuelo. "Nothing but junkies and faggots out at this hour." This was California in the 1980s, but I had grown up hearing the same warnings from my grandparents in Michoacán.

There was no asking about these matters at home. Or rather, I didn't dare ask, afraid that opening this topic of conversation would lead to questions, and upon further inquiry the eventual discovery that I was a homosexual, that I might have this deadly touch that threatened them all.

I understood, however, that as a gay man I wasn't born with AIDS. But somehow it would blossom in my body, a type of puberty that occurred when a person came out of the closet. To keep AIDS at bay, I remained safely hidden. By my twisted logic, I could have sex with men, but I wasn't gay; therefore, I would not contract the disease.

The other relief I had was that when those late-night news programs like 20/20 featured people succumbing to AIDS, they were all white men in cities I had never been to—New York, San Francisco, Chicago, Los Angeles. I was a Mexican in the Coachella Valley and I was not yet gay. I was free to sneak into the beds of other men and orgasm quietly beneath the sheets, the sticky fluid wiped clean with my underwear, which I would push to the bottom of the hamper when I got home.

There was no discussion of safe sex. In fact, there was no discussion of anything. The entire courtship took place with a look and a smile, a gesture and caress. If neither of us said anything, then no one would really know what kind of pleasure had taken place. Exiting the neighbor's house down the street was like waking up from a dream. Whatever evidence of intimacy evaporated, except for the excited heartbeat, which was neither visible nor audible.

The white gays of the city met in public places—bars and bathhouses, bus depot bathrooms, park benches and park bushes—their hunger on full display. Our Mexican housing project had none of these things. The only words of caution delivered to us high schoolers were "Don't get pregnant" and "Don't get a girl pregnant." No one ever said, "Don't get AIDS." It must be, I deduced, because that was not an actual danger here.

Public figures who died of AIDS were also white gays. First there was Rock Hudson in 1985. And then Liberace in 1987. Both outed only after their deaths. I was living in the town of Indio at the time, not far from Palm Springs, where Liberace took his final breath. I couldn't stop thinking of the teacher in health class who had remarked, "If you diet, do it responsibly. Don't do it like Liberace and his watermelon-only meals. Watermelon is 92 percent water. He's going to starve to death." No one had to be convinced that Liberace was gay. But Rock Hudson?

"You would never know, watching all those Doris Day movies," said one of my female friends.

I was about to say that I too felt the loss of this beautiful man but stopped myself in time. I kept my crush on Rock Hudson a secret, like I did everything else. My adolescent desire was burning a hole in my pants and I was afraid to give myself away.

Still, AIDS seemed very far from my everyday reality. It was not perceived as a hazard but as a joke even long after I graduated from high school. There was that banda song "La ruca no era ruca" (The chick wasn't a chick), whose catchy tune became popular on the radio in the 1990s. The story: A Chicano gives a ride to a pretty blonde but realizes his mistake when she starts to seduce him. The chick was not a chick; she turned out to be a dude. "Squeeze me, homeboy," she says. And the homeboy replies, "No, because my wrist will go limp." And then, "Give me a kiss, homeboy," to which the homeboy says, "No, because you'll give me AIDS." And then that atrocious pun:

Hombre con mujer? No da. (Man with a woman? No infection.)

Hombre con hombre? Sí da. (Man with a man? AIDS.)

The pun would make its way into those silly movies with drunk losers stumbling down the street on their way to the brothels. As long as the whores were not transvestites, there was nothing to fear.

What saved me from becoming HIV positive as a teenager, except sheer luck? The ignorance and misinformation about AIDS were rampant in my community. The first people I met who were HIV positive were a white woman who visited my biology class in college and a young white man who spoke out at a rally on campus. Both pale, blue-eyed, and dirty blonde. I couldn't see myself in either of them. When the biology professor embraced the young woman, I confirmed that my community's belief that AIDS could be transmitted through touch was stupid and wrong.

But that eye-opening moment was still years away. Until then I had to walk among my peers who shouted insults at the guys who dressed like the members of Duran Duran—feathery hair beneath hats, eyeliner, jackets over T-shirts, and ankle boots.

"They're gays," high schoolers said with the same disinterested tone they used when they pointed to a group of students in the distance and said, "They're sophomores."

They were gays but no one was afraid of them. Meaning, they didn't have AIDS, or rather that AIDS didn't exist where we lived. It was a plague that thrived in places too remote to concern us. We moved about carefree and careless, side-eying the girls who got pregnant and had to drop out of school.

I wasn't exactly curious about the disease either because I was rarely reminded of it, except by those after-hours reports that were too dull and too educational to attract a young audience. I watched them because I wanted to see what gays looked like. The only one I was familiar with was the one in the mirror. The Duran Duran groupies, I deduced, were not gay; they were just different. The real gays were on TV, dying before our eyes.

Their startling thinness, sunken eyes, and aggrieved expressions moved me to tears. I felt sorry for the certainty of their deaths, but I was saddened even more that their bodies were being punished for their unavoidable desire. The damage was exacerbated by the fact that they became exiled from the rest of society and disowned by their loved ones.

I came across one notable exception. The parents of a man suffering from AIDS were being interviewed. The household had gone bankrupt trying to meet the expense of the treatments, which were still experimental then. Father and mother sat in two chairs, their hands on their laps, while the son was prone in the top mattress of a bunk bed. Only his head resting on his arm was visible. He wasn't hiding. He was simply weak, defeated.

"Will you stand by your son to the very end?" the reporter asked.

The father took a deep breath and said, "We don't have quitters in this family. Right, Jackie?"

From the recesses of this scene, a solemn voice responded like an object dropping to the floor in the other room. "Right," Jackie said.

The mother stared blankly at the camera. She had nothing left to say.

I was relieved for Jackie. His blessing was having parents who didn't abandon him. I didn't trust my community or my family to respond the same way. I simply let that part of me dissolve into the everyday heterosexuality I already lived in. That meant tolerating the teasing of the aunties who were always matchmaking whenever the neighbors walked past, arm in arm with their pubescent daughters.

"Rigo should marry Doña Domitila's youngest," one said.

"Oh no, that's a terrible choice," the other said. "Doña Domitila would make a horrible mother-in-law."

"You're right," the first agreed. "Too involved with her children. How about Doña Rosita's girl? She's already a teenager by now."

"But she walks funny. Pigeon-toed, I think."

Straightness was out in the open, uncomplicated and natural. What I had was secretive and shameful. I wasn't sure I even had a word for it. All the ones tossed out by my cousins and friends were charged with derision and hatred. Only on one occasion was the topic of homosexuality not shot down with contempt.

"They say guys turn gay if women don't give them the time of day," a young man said once. This was in Mexicali during summer. The guys had gathered in the evening around a small fire to tell stories and make jokes. That statement made everyone go so quiet that suddenly the crackling of the wood became loud. They stared intently into the flames until someone finally broke the uncomfortable silence with a laugh-inducing fart.

That moment stayed with me because I sensed that that young man was trying to reveal something about himself. But such an admission was not going to find a sympathetic ear in this gathering of male adolescents who liked to talk dirty and shove their stinky socks into each other's noses. If anyone was willing to listen, it was me. I too didn't understand the origin of my desire. But I was too afraid to disclose my doubts and insecurities about sexuality, especially to this crowd, most of them my cousins.

I never saw that young man again. Maybe he was never invited to join the group again. Maybe he made that decision on his own. Or maybe, I said to myself to ease my own guilt, he was no longer adrift but had found the shore he was looking for.

On another occasion, I was working on the layout of *Sandscripts* by myself. The young man who sat at the same table I did in English class must have seen me as he walked by.

"Whatcha doing?" he asked as he stepped into the classroom. He was not particularly attractive. In fact, of the guys who sat with me at the table, he was the one I glanced at the least. He was too skinny and pale, and was the rudest of the bunch, tossing balls of paper at the table of overachievers, who ignored him and never dared complain to the teacher.

"I'm working on the next issue of the newspaper," I answered, and kept to my task.

"That's nice," he said.

There was something chilling about the way he said that. A strange combination of condescension and ridicule. He had pitched his voice a bit higher, which I knew was a mocking imitation of my own voice. I swallowed hard and kept focused. One thing I had learned about bullies was that they didn't let something go if they knew it was inflicting discomfort or pain.

A strange silence filled the room, except for the sound of my pencil drawing lines along the side of the metal ruler. I shifted my body to see what he was doing. I didn't want to be surprised by a flying object. My body froze and immediately I began to sweat. He was arousing himself. The outline of his erection was quite visible beneath his pants.

I wasn't sure if this was an invitation or a trap, something he would use to torment me for the rest of the school year.

"You can do what you want with it," he said. This time his voice struck a different timbre altogether. It was more of a seductive whisper.

I was no stranger to men's penises. But I had only slept with Mexican men, not white ones. That's when those images came flooding out of my brain. The anxious mouths, the skeletal frames, the sunken eyes, the dark bruises on that colorless flesh. *This is how I get AIDS*, I thought to myself. *This is how I die.* The sweat came pouring down on the paper layout, blurring the perfect pencil lines. I turned my head, nauseous and dizzy. I began to shake, rattling the ruler on the table.

He must have seen how close to a seizure I was that he did something I had not thought him capable of: he took pity on me.

"Hey," he said. "It's alright. I'm not going to hurt you."

He rose from his seat and placed his arm on my back, tapping lightly, the way my mother used to do when she had me bend over a pan of hot water and VapoRub, a towel over my head and the pot so that the fumes could clear my sinuses. Her touch was reassuring and gave me the strength to hold my pose.

I began to cry. I had done wrong to this young man, despite his initial act. I had just demonstrated the most homophobic reaction. And in the end, he didn't want to hurt me, not really. He wanted me to see in him something he saw in himself or something he saw in me. And what did I see in myself but a clandestine lover who surrendered to the closeted men in the neighborhood because only in the dark and only for a moment could we experience our true selves.

His tenderness consumed me. I wanted to tell him I didn't deserve it. I wanted to let him know what a coward and complete asshole I was to project on him what I feared the most—a sickness that I knew I was susceptible to, especially in my Catholic community because none of us used condoms, but that was okay because only the white gays and junkies got AIDS.

But I didn't tell him anything. I stopped the sobbing and the shaking. And he appeared relieved. Neither of us wanted this moment to move past the lunch hour. The bell was about to ring, and everyone would come rushing in.

"You okay?" he asked.

"I'm okay," I said.

Those were the last words we ever said to each other. During English class, he returned to being that troublemaker in the back of the room. Though I noticed that he never picked on me again. I avoided eye contact as much as I could. But once in a while I glanced over. And if he caught me looking, I turned my gaze immediately.

Graduation was within view. Senioritis was widespread because we were anxious to grow up and take our first taste of independence. I too was itching to leave the school, the town, the neighborhood, my house. I was going away to college like many others. I was off to discover all those things never discussed by either my high school teachers or my family.

Less than a year later, I would have my first sexual experience in college. When my date pulled out a condom from his backpack, I stared at it with amazement. We were still calling them rubbers at the time, just like the horny teenagers in the slasher flicks. "We don't want to make any babies," he jokingly said. I must have chuckled, but it was tinged with disappointment that, in 1989, we were still not acknowledging the real purpose for protection.

A Box of Ash

Color azúl. You say blue, like sky. We say chupipiti. Y cielo
es auanda.

—Abuela's lessons in Purépecha

MÉXICO'S NATIONAL ELECTIONS are held every six years on the first Sunday in July. Since I traveled to my homeland during the summers, my visits were bound to overlap with the period when propaganda was painted onto any available mural. The telltale Mexican flag–colored seals of its competing political parties—PRI, PAN, and PRD—were everywhere, particularly on the walls that faced Highway 15, which connected Morelia to Zacapu. I aimed to be in México during that time because July was my birthday month, and because I wanted to be out of the U.S. during the Fourth of July and the artifice of its patriotic fervor.

In 2000, the year that Vicente Fox, a PAN candidate, broke the seventy-one-year rule of the PRI, my relatives on my mother's side, the more conservative branch of my family tree, celebrated the win. I had thought naively that this was a good thing, until my socially conscious friends informed me that this was a right-wing party. Six years later, Felipe Calderón, also a PAN candidate, maintained that rule. My family was ecstatic. Not only was Calderón also a conservative, but he was a son of Michoacán, born in the state capital, Morelia.

I was in México during Calderón's win. I witnessed the shouting matches in the plaza rallies between opposing sides and the clashes between bystanders and those marching in parades, proudly waving their party's name spray-painted on white sheets. My friends weren't loyal to either party. I was privy to many a discussion about how corrupt all politicians were, and that what this country needed was another revolution. They usually kept these conversations private, but when the election results of 2006 were announced in the car radio as we were driving home after an evening out, they took it upon themselves to hurl insults at the celebrants, who in turn yelled back with equal disdain. Mortified, I sunk into the back seat, praying that we wouldn't start getting rocks or glass bottles thrown at us.

In 2018 I arrived in México completely ignorant of the fact that it was an election year. But as soon as I climbed on the bus to travel from Morelia to Zacapu, there were the freshly painted signs all along the route letting me know the political drama was about to unfold. Ernesto Peña Nieto, a PRI candidate, had broken the twelve-year PAN rule in 2012. This was a decisive election to see whether the PRI could hold on to its power or whether the PAN would rattle the cages again.

Mexican elections didn't concern me much because they didn't affect me, and because, like many Mexicans, I had become cynical of the Mexican government, disillusioned that any president would be able to control the true leaders of this part of the country, the drug lords. In fact, it was rumored that the government was in league with the cartels. It didn't matter what party ruled when the murders and kidnappings persisted with impunity. As my revolutionary friends would say, "Same soup, different bowl." I had done zero research on the Mexican candidates, but everywhere I turned I saw the acronym AMLO (Andrés Manuel López Obrador), representing the PRI. I resolved to look him up once I returned to the states.

I had a different purpose for visiting what was considered a dangerous drug cartel terrain. I wanted to move my mother's remains and place them inside the crypt of Zacapu's most glorious church, la Parroquia de Santa Ana.

La Parroquia de Santa Ana was founded at the same time as the town was established in 1548. In fact, a church is what usually marks the start of Spanish colonial rule. There's no turning back from Catholicism and its tenets once the Franciscan monks take root in Indigenous territory, making it their religious domain. Zacapu was the perfect place to do this because, as the town liked to boast, it was once the heart of the Purépecha empire.

The town name came from the word tsakapu, which meant rock. Take possession of the heart and the rest begins to crumble.

When the bus finally turned toward the station at the center of town, I was seized by the pang of nostalgia, even though I had visited the year before. These were the streets of my childhood in a place that didn't look very different after all these years. It was like stepping into the photographs of the past. When one of the passengers called out, "Thank God we're home!" my eyes became watery. I pulled the protective window curtain back, as did many others, and soaked in the familiar sights: the light-green paint that was popular for coating the walls of corner stores, laborers traveling to work on bicycle, women sweeping the sidewalks and tossing mop water into the streets by swinging red or yellow plastic buckets, the crowing roosters, and the gas tank truck dragging a chain with a metal ring that clinked on the cobblestones to alert the clientele.

Zacapu was a sprawling town whose summer temperature dropped at night into the mornings but rose steadily through the day. All those sweaters and denim jackets on people out and about vanished by noon. It was not yet 9 a.m. I zipped my black hoodie up to my neck as I exited the bus.

As was my custom, my first stop was Panteón San Franciscano to pay my respects to the ancestors. I was prepared for the worse when I walked up to my mother's grave. I got word from one of my cousins that her father, Tío Chuy, had wanted to let me know that another grave now lay on top.

Cemetery real estate in Zacapu was precious, particularly in this cemetery because it was the oldest, but it couldn't grow past the walls. Now it was growing vertically.

"Whoever owns the plot can decide whoever they want to bury there," Tío Chuy had stated. "The grave is now a high-rise."

Indeed, the tombs were stacked atop each other. Underground was Abuela Herminia's aunt. When my mother died in 1982, the aunt's family had graciously agreed to let us place her tomb above ground. In its early years, the tomb looked oddly pretty with its light-blue tile and a large concrete sculpture of an opened book with her name written in the pages. Eventually the tiles started to chip and the book became weather-worn with the lettering stained and darkened after years of exposure to rain and heat. When another relative died—a girl I never met—that small tomb was laid across my mother's feet. It looked strange, but somehow, I found it touching, as if my mother were watching over this young cousin who had also been taken too soon. But the breaking point came when La Borrega, my colorful cousin, joined the group burial.

La Borrega was the family derelict. His close relations tried repeatedly to clean him up and get him to sleep anywhere except the streets, which is where he chose to live when he wasn't drunk. I always suspected it was less a concern for his well-being than the fact that his appearance—disheveled and urine-drenched—embarrassed his mother in particular, who had to cross the street in order to avoid him on her way to church. But La Borrega recognized her, no matter how much she tried to hide beneath her rebozo, and called out to her, "Amáaaaaaaa," a bleating sound that reminded people of a sheep, which is why that nickname, La Borrega, stuck. My mother's family didn't mention him, though I recall Abuela Herminia pulling me back when we passed him on the sidewalk one day and he called out, "Tíaaaaaaa." I was about thirteen years old at the time, and I knew better than to ask questions. I kept my gaze fixed forward.

I also knew that I had met this man before when I was a child of six or seven. That many years ago he was already a lost cause. When he staggered up the street, he became easy fodder for the kids, who seized any opportunity for fun. I joined the group that came up behind him and called out, "Put your hands up!" And when he complied, we added, "Now put your feet up!" And he would march, lifting his knees up to his belly.

That same man who had surrendered his life to alcohol, becoming the village clown and family shame, was now resting on top of my mother. I understood my uncle's urgency. He wanted me to come down and cover the expense of removing her from the cemetery, cremating her remains, and then placing her in the church crypt. After I saw the outrageous state of this high-rise grave, I was determined to get it done.

Since I wanted to avoid drawing any unnecessary attention to myself, I had arrived with one day's notice. The plan was to take care of as much as I could in one day, before anyone with malicious intent found out I had come from the U.S. and then plotted my kidnapping for ransom, or worse, the kidnapping of one of my close relatives. These were the new realities of the homeland.

I walked to my grandparents' house near the intersection of Río Bravo and Río Rodano, uphill from the cemetery. The grid of streets, all named after rivers, was easy to navigate. The houses too looked unchanged. But the streets were now paved. Gone were the old cobblestones that caused many a person to trip. None of the neighbors would recognize me anymore, and very few people I walked past even acknowledged me. In my youth, when I walked with Abuela Herminia to Mercado Morelos, where Abuelo Melecio worked unloading the fruits and vegetables from the cargo trucks until his body gave out, I would be reprimanded for not saying "Buenos días" or "Buenas tardes" to those we crossed paths with.

When I reached the house, which had steep concrete stairs to the entrance, I thought about how dangerous it had become for my aging grandparents, Abuelo Melecio in his nineties and Abuela Herminia in her late eighties, both suffering from dementia and he moving about on two crutches. They still had a hearty appetite, though, which is why Tío Chuy was certain they would outlive us all.

"You know, the doctor once said my father needed emergency surgery to remove a cyst in his stomach. But there was no guarantee he would survive it. Well, we opted to let him live with it as long as he could."

"It's probably for the best," I said.

Abuelo Melecio sat on the couch with his hat on, looking at me once in a while as if trying to recognize me. Abuela's condition had worsened since the previous year, when I was last here. She spent most of the time fading in and out of lucidness. She kept repeating "And who are you?" every fifteen minutes or so, and it broke my heart each time.

"Well, the doctor was a fool," Tío Chuy said.

"Why is that?" I asked.

"That doctor died a few years ago."

We laughed it off. But I wanted to get to the matter at hand. I changed the subject.

"How's the situation with the cartels?" I asked Tío Chuy.

"Well, every week there are still bodies," he said. "But they're chopping each other's heads off, you know. The rest of us just need to stay out of the way."

"That's horrible," I said. I couldn't stomach the thought of decapitated corpses, though that was what the headlines kept screaming about. It made me want to rush out of town as soon as I could.

"I made inquiries," Tío Chuy said. "But if you want to do all this in one day, there's only one method." He made a hand gesture that implied holding a thick wad of cash.

I sent myself $800 through Western Union and the bribing began.

"Now's the time to do it," Tío Chuy said as he drove me in his beat-up Pinto. "It's before the elections. Administrators want to hoard cash before they get replaced."

Our first stop was at the funeral home, which would take charge of the exhumation and transportation of the ashes to the church. Thankfully, we didn't have to walk into the display room with its walls lined with caskets. For our purpose we entered a small office with a cluttered desk. The administrator was surprisingly young, dressed in a white dress shirt and navy-blue pants. Since Tío Chuy was the older one, the administrator directed his attention to him.

After Tío Chuy explained what we needed and how quickly we wanted it done, the young man said it was impossible. These things took time, he said. It was a lengthy and complicated process. There was paperwork involved, and signatures. The whole affair would take at least a month. This was a busy office, after all. He reached over and thumbed through the stacks of folders on his desk for effect. But when Tío Chuy offered him the obligatory mordida—the bribe—his disposition changed.

"But I can certainly cut through all that, of course, seeing as how this gentleman traveled from far away. May I interest you in picking out the urn?"

After browsing a few pages of photographs in an album, I opted for something simple but elegant: a dark wood urn with an ornate gilded cross on the upper-right side and a plaque in the lower-left side, which would bear my mother's name.

"There's just one thing I need first: a signature on this permit from the cemetery officials," he said, handing us a document.

As we drove to the cemetery, which was only a few blocks away, Tío Chuy shook his head.

"México will never change," he said. "Just watch: it's a whole network of crooked dealings, even for something like this."

The small, dark office in the cemetery was like a tomb itself, with very little ventilation and a weak light that might have well been a candle. The official, an older gentleman with a pair of glasses that looked like they had been pulled out of a 1970s catalog, also informed us that it was a lengthy and complicated process. There was a queue, of course, and scheduling was always a hassle.

I almost laughed out loud at the theater of these exchanges, remembering how my own family would gripe about the privileges of the wealthy. Money was the key that opened any door.

"Perhaps we can offer compensation for speeding up the process," Tío Chuy said, and the official didn't have to work hard to decipher the code.

"There's just one thing, however," he said as gave us another piece of paper. "You need a signature from the original owners of the plot."

Tío Chuy drove around the corner to the mercado, where he and his wife ran a small bodega. She shook her head at the ridiculousness of it all and then handed me a pen.

"What is this for?" I asked. "For the owner of the plot?"

Tío Chuy laughed. "The owner of the plot isn't even alive anymore, and her children are scattered all over the state."

"What are we going to do, then?" I asked naively.

"You're going to sign it," he said.

We dropped off the document at the cemetery. And once the official signed the administrator's document, we delivered it to the funeral home. Everything was getting done efficiently. We hit a snag, however, when he inquired about placing my mother's urn at la Parroquia de Santa Ana. The crypt was at full capacity. We thought this was an invitation to bribe, but it didn't work.

"I'm sorry," the woman in the church offices said. "You can try la Parroquia del Perpetuo Socorro in Colonia Anáhuac. It's a newer church not far from here. There's likely plenty of space there."

La Parroquia del Perpetuo Socorro did not impress me, but it would have to do. The outside was modern and angular, nothing close to the colonial architecture and beauty of la Parroquia de Santa Ana. The interior was lovely, however. The high ceilings, the majestic altar, and the light wood of the pews—everything was clean and polished because this was, indeed, a new construction.

The crypt was hidden behind one of the walls with a large swinging door. It was not what I expected. The compartments were stacked together neatly, each visible surface like a piece of a puzzle that had been completed to showcase the large image of la Virgen de Guadalupe. There was very little somber or mausoleum-like about it. It was actually bright and, for lack of a better word, joyful. I was convinced then that this was the right resting place for my mother's ashes.

When we approached the clerk, an older lady with a perm, she was quick with the script.

"The issue is that you are not members of our church," she said. "The crypt is reserved for this community's congregation. To make an exception requires a lengthy and complicated process. There's an application, of course, and we do expect members of the family to attend our services."

Exhausted of the politeness of this game, I laid a stack of bills on the desk.

Without missing a beat, the woman said: "Did you take a look? Would you like a spot in the higher section or the lower section? I suggest the lower—that way you can place a vase with flowers on the floor."

I chose a compartment at the bottom. As it turned out, there was room in there for four urns. Tío Chuy asked if it would be okay to place my grandparents' ashes there when their time came, and I assented. The fourth spot, however, would be reserved for either my brother or me.

Once everything was in order, Tío Chuy promised to see the whole process through and to send me pictures. A few weeks later, he did better than that: he sent me a video of the ceremonial mass. All of my mother's siblings were present, along with Abuela Herminia, who seemed confused about the whole affair. They chose to print my mother's maiden name, Avelina Alcalá Hernández, in the small plaque on the box, which annoyed me because I thought this was disrespectful to my father. But the inscription on the crypt itself read: Familia González Alcalá.

The real star of the video, however, was the altar boy with his bottle-thick glasses and cowlick. He was like a character in a Cantinflas movie. He was adorable and diligent in his task, which was to hold the small silver pot that contained the holy water and the blessing wand.

Before I headed back to Morelia, this time by taxi, I sat with my grandparents having a meal: pork in red sauce with beans and rice. Tío Chuy was correct; they did have a hearty appetite. He stood nearby, however, because he didn't want them to fight over the tortillas.

I wasn't sure what was a crueler fate: Abuelo Ramón and Abuela María were dead, freed of their respective illnesses; Abuelo Melecio and Abuela Herminia were still alive, but no matter how close I sat near them, their memories and minds were leagues away. Abuela Herminia in particular dejected me. Suddenly I saw a flash of recognition in her eyes when she looked at me. I tried to coax it out of her.

"Do you know who I am?"

"No," she answered between bites. "Who are you?"

"I'm Avelina's son," I said.

"Avelina?" she wondered. She looked at my grandfather. "Didn't Avelina have daughters?"

Abuelo Melecio answered slowly, "No. She had sons."

"Sons?" Abuela Herminia said. "Where are they?"

Abuelo Melecio didn't answer. Either he didn't want to startle her by telling her that one of them was sitting right in front of her or he didn't have a clue either.

I didn't bother saying good-bye to my grandparents. I simply walked out for one last ride in the old Pinto. Tío Chuy was dropping me off at the taxi stand. Once inside the taxi, in a spurt of spontaneity, I decided to stop in Quiroga, the halfway point between Zacapu and Morelia. I had the urge for carnitas, Michoacán style, and Quiroga was the place to get them.

I would have to spend the night, however, since carnitas were sold in the mornings.

After a day of rushing from one place to another, I took a deep breath. It was time to get back to me.

In Quiroga, I checked into the Hotel Tarasco. I dropped my bag in my room and headed out to soak in the afternoon vibe of the crowded streets and tourist shops. This was one of Abuelo Ramón's favorite places to visit. He was the grandparent I liked the least, yet he had a palate that never let him cook or eat anything mediocre. I was honoring that palate, and the times he brought my brother and me to Michoacán. It was because of him, I had to admit, that my bond remained tight with the homeland.

I told my brother about the day's events when I sat in the town square, listening to a Purépecha band play pirekuas on a stage. Abuela María would have been in paradise, maybe even daring to dance like the uáhri she was, slowly bouncing up and down while shuffling her feet back and forth and side to side.

"How do we decide who goes into the crypt?" I asked him. "Whichever one of us dies first?"

The question lingered heavily in the air. I was older by one and a half years, but my brother was suffering from more health issues than I was.

"I guess you," he said. "I want my ashes to be cast out to the sea."

Such a burial made sense for my brother, whose passion was fishing. He had spent countless hours on the shore or on boats. Catching a fish or two was a nice reward, but it was the peace he found in the middle of the water that he looked forward to. I had found such refuge in my travels alone. Viejo San Juan in Puerto Rico and Oaxaca de Juárez were my two havens, and I went as often as I could. Although we would ultimately find rest in our deaths, we had to find it among the chaos of the living while we were still here.

"Then you or your children will have to bring my ashes," I said. "That's all I ask of any of you."

After the call, I wondered if I could do the same with Abuela María's remains—have them exhumed and cremated in order to bring her back to her homeland. The process would be as bureaucratic as it was here, but without the possibility of shortcuts. I assumed Tía Melania would have a say in the matter, and I couldn't picture her cosigning on anything that involved disturbing Abuela's resting place. Could I convince my cousins to appeal to her?

When we were young, trying to figure out what to give our mothers for Mother's Day, we had to get creative because we didn't have any money. We thought about going into the desert and collecting wildflowers for bouquets, but the only desert within walking distance was the dump full of weeds and dry brush. We thought about singing them a song (the oldest cousin on guitar), but some of us thought that was too corny and others said they were too timid to sing.

Finally, it came to us. We would give them a scratcher, now that the Lotto had become a thing in California. All the adults loved scratchers. Tío Ramón was old enough to purchase one. We gathered our change and presented it to him. He rolled his eyes.

"This is stupid," he said. "Use your head. Would you rather have all these women fighting over the prize money or have one woman—the only one that we can trust, my mother—decide who gets how much?"

Somehow it made sense, though as soon as Tío Ramón set off on his bike to the gas station down the street, we began to suspect that there was something in it for him if Abuela did indeed win. Or worse, something for Abuelo.

That afternoon, we presented the scratcher to Abuela with a piece of paper signed by all ten grandchildren, but we wished all our mothers a Happy Mother's Day. While Abuela began scratching, all of us kids gathered in a room and chanted, "Let Abuela win. Let Abuela win. Let Abuela win." Nothing came of it, except that we had made it clear that we held our Abuela in much higher esteem than we did the women who had given birth to us.

Would my cousins still feel the same after all these years? Would they back me up on this wild idea of mine to bring Abuela home? I needed to mull it over some more before contacting any of them, those who were still living.

The evening chill was upon me. I bought a cup of cinnamon tea from a lady behind the stands of food. A minute later I stopped a woman selling sweet breads out of a plastic bucket.

"Do you have puerquitos?" I asked. These pig-shaped cookies were a specialty in Michoacán. I was surprised that the bakeries in Oaxaca didn't make them. When I asked why, the baker simply said, "They're not a thing here."

I bought whatever the woman had left in her bucket. The evening came to a close with me, a tourist in my homeland, chewing on a bread while sitting on a bench in Quiroga. The band sang another song, accompanied by the guitar and a pair of violins.

After a while of sitting in the small park, I was approached by a young Indigenous man who smiled at me and then took a seat on the end of the bench. As a tourist traveling alone in Europe or the Americas, I was familiar with this tactic. A man on his own attracted sex workers, drug dealers, and scam artists but also romantic interest from gay men who were either closeted or out for a quick fling. Gay tourists were convenient for these encounters because they were not sticking around too long, they likely didn't know many people in town to tell, and most importantly, they could host in their hotel. In places like Quiroga, bachelors still lived at home.

In my travels, if I felt lonely, I might engage such men in conversation, and maybe, if the desire was mutual, I wouldn't be shy about inviting company back to my hotel. Most times, however, I would ask the person to join me for a meal, and it felt great to have a conversation over dinner instead of scrolling through the Internet on my phone by myself as I waited to be served.

Since this young man was Indigenous, I didn't want to reject him too swiftly. I decided to be kind and eventually let him down gently since I was not interested in sex that evening, not after the day I had just experienced in Zacapu.

"I'm Janitzio," he said, holding out his hand.

I shook it and chuckled. "Janitzio, as in the island in the middle of el lago de Pátzcuaro?"

"Yes," he said. "It means—"

"Place of rain, place to fish," I said, cutting him off. "I know. My grandmother was Purépecha. I'm Rigoberto."

"Nice to meet you, Rigoberto," he said, and then he gave me a sheepish smile. "You know, Janitzio also means corn silk."

I looked at his pitch-black hair. "Well, yours looks like it's soft as corn silk, but they missed the mark in terms of color."

That flirty exchange broke the ice, and for the moment I was convinced that this conversation would not become transactional. Janitzio was about fifteen years younger than me. We were the same height, but our frames were quite different: he was slim and I was husky. The Purépecha band was retiring now that night was setting and there wasn't much light in the park. Also, the temperature was dropping.

"I could use a soup or something," I said. "What's the nicest place nearby?"

"Atzimba. It's just a block down the street," he said. "Do you know what Atzimba means?"

"I don't." We both rose from the bench, and I followed his lead.

He looked back at me. "Beautiful princess."

The restaurant looked elegant with its Moorish tiles and tablecloths in bright red and yellow. The entrance corridor was lined with large potted plants. Business was slow that evening, though a pair of waiters, charming older gentlemen dressed in guayaberas, moved with grace from one room of the restaurant to the next. To combat the cold we ordered fish soup, but since I saw charales on the menu, I asked for an order of the deep-fried salty fish as well.

"I haven't had charales since I visited Janitzio when I was younger," I said once they arrived.

"Well, now that you're older you're having them *with* Janitzio," he responded.

Since he had won me over, our conversation at dinner covered a wide territory, from chit-chat about the upcoming presidential election to the difficulties of our present situations. I told him I had come to Michoacán to move my mother's remains to the church but spared him the details about the briberies. He told me he was studying to be a pharmacist in Morelia, but everything changed when his parents went north to Utah and left him taking care of his aging grandmother, Erendira. Erendira meant happy in Purépecha.

"They send money regularly," he explained. "But they're undocumented. They can't come back. They've been gone for over a decade."

"Why were you asked to be her caretaker?" I said.

"Because I was the unmarried one," he said. "Everyone else had their own families and obligations, and Nana didn't want to leave her house."

I didn't have to ask if his family didn't think he would ever marry because I understood how these arrangements became convenient, for the bachelor as well because now he had an excuse for his single status.

We ate in silence for the next few minutes. The reality of our journeys hovered above us, darkening the mood and our enjoyment of the meal. I stirred the spoon in the bowl slower and slower each time. The events of that day were finally setting in, and I felt sluggish.

"I'm tired," I said. "Tomorrow I'm getting up early and then heading to Morelia."

"I wish I could go with you," he said. "It'll be a while before I see anything outside of Quiroga."

I wasn't sure how to respond. Each time I came to México, I came across these stories of families separated because crossing the border was taking a chance in a promised land. And also, stories of gay men who had been left behind, like Janitizio, or who had fled, like me.

"Well, it was wonderful meeting you, Janitzio," I said. I didn't mention anything about staying in touch because it would come across as disingenuous.

I paid the bill and Janitzio walked me back to the hotel. At the entrance, where a pair of life-sized Purépecha mannequins in traditional dress stood greeting the guests, I turned around to shake his hand.

"Do you mind if I come up with you?" he asked.

I hesitated. "Honestly, I wasn't seeking company tonight."

"No, nothing like that," Janitzio said. "Innocent, I promise."

We walked up two flights of stairs to my room. Hotel Tarasco had display cases embedded into the walls of the hallways. A heavy key unlocked the heavy door. My room was small but quaint. A little TV looked down from its perch in the top corner.

"I wanted to give you a proper hug," he said. He took a step forward and wrapped his arms around me, and I did the same.

There was nothing erotic about the embrace. It felt like a release, a letting down of our guard in a culture that policed our queer behavior in public. I don't know which of us began to weep first. It didn't matter. We needed that moment to unravel the knots of grief in our bodies. I couldn't even say what I was crying about, there was too much sadness to choose from. But this unburdening was necessary.

"How do you say thank you in Purépecha?" I asked.

"Diosï meyamu," said Janitzio.

"Diosï meyamu," I repeated. Abuela's Purépecha lessons never reached the stage of commonly used phrases.

"I hope our paths cross again," I said, sounding more sentimental than I had intended.

I had a feeling I said one thing too much, that I should have left it at thank you. Janitzio smiled, and for a moment I thought I recognized Abuela's smile, a deep crescent that reminded me of the song "Janitzio." It was much too late in the moment to bring up the song made famous by the late Lola Beltrán and composed by the great Agustín Lara. But the lines that grabbed me every time were "como brilla la luna sobre el lago de cristal, así brillan tus ojos cuando acaban de llorar" (just as the moon shimmers over the crystal lake, so too do your eyes shine brightly after they finish crying).

"Éskari sésï níntaaka," he said. "Safe travels."

Janitzio left and I got ready for bed. The streets had quieted down now that the tourist shops had closed. The town would be buzzing with energy early in the morning, when the carnitas sellers set up their stands in front of the park. I had something to look forward to before leaving Quiroga.

As I drifted to sleep, my grandparents, my mother, Janitzio, and many other thoughts were swirling in my head, though none of them was going to keep me awake that night. I had squeezed a long journey into a single day. One second, I'm picking out my mother's urn, and the next I'm holding a Purépecha kindred spirit in my arms. The cycle of life and death spun around me a few times.

My mind did snag on one thought before I dozed off: *Did Abuela ever visit her mother's grave? Or her father's?* During our visits in Abuelo's truck, and even that time we walked into el Panteón San Franciscano, Abuela didn't mention Mamá Lola or Papá Juan. Where were they buried? Maybe Nahuatzen. Maybe Cherán. I had no one to ask. But unlike Abuela, Mamá Lola and Papá Juan were resting in their Purépecha homeland.

The next day, my hearty breakfast awaited me before heading back to Morelia. I felt safer there among the crowds because I was anonymous. If anyone asked, I just said I was visiting from La Paz, where my brother lived. Whether or not they believed me didn't matter much, as long as no one could trace me back to Zacapu, which made my family vulnerable.

In a matter of weeks, the election would be decided and AMLO would win, bringing a fresh wave of optimism to the citizens of México. Perhaps he would do what the previous presidents had not: shut down the cartels. He would impress my revolutionary friends as well when, during his inauguration, he received blessings from an Indigenous leader. Perhaps the tensions between the Mexican government and the Indigenous community would also begin to heal. I had my doubts about all of it. There was no certainty about anything in México anymore, except for death. And carnitas.

Separation

Rojo. Red, like blood. Charhapiti. Sangre es iurhíri.

—Abuela's lessons in Purépecha

IN THE LAST YEAR OF HER LIFE, Abuela had become increasingly paranoid and difficult for my brother, who lived next door, to deal with. She still had to trust him with her ATM card to get cash for her when he crossed the border to California for work, but she would also accuse him of stealing from her. And when he confronted her, asking her to take the card and find someone else to do her the favor, she took back her words, but only until the next cash withdrawal. Nevertheless, Alex put up with it. She was our grandmother, after all, the woman who had taken us in when we became orphans because our mother had died and our father had run off to get married again.

I reminded my brother of this, though he didn't need it. And I tried not to make it sound like a reprimand because the truth was, I had the privilege of staying away from all the problems that still plagued the family. My brother had his own family to contend with. I was still single and traveling the world on my own, reporting back to my brother after each trip. He, on the other hand, had a difficult work schedule as the manager of a gas station across the border. He had his wife, daughter, and newborn son. And Abuela.

My sister-in-law, Lupe, was less tolerant and had no problem going up to Abuela and asking her why she said the things she said. Namely, that my brother's wife was lazy and that she talked behind his back and didn't take good care of the house.

"Mind your own business, señora," she told her.

They informed me of all these things when I visited from New York City. I bit my tongue, even though I thought this complaint was disrespectful.

Since the death of Abuelo, Abuela had become more reclusive, refusing to let anyone into her house except for my father, who sometimes spent the night. Otherwise she was content to be alone with her motley collection of stray dogs that barked at anything that stirred. This arrangement worked out until her health started failing.

"Lupe found her roaming around the yard," Alex explained over our weekly phone call. "We thought she might have had a stroke or something. When I got home from work, we took her to the hospital."

"What was wrong?" I asked.

"Well, the doctor was pissed. He started yelling at us, accusing us of neglect. Abuela hadn't been taking her medication and her blood pressure had skyrocketed. He said she could have died, Turrútut."

"But it's not your fault," I said.

Then who's is it? We had let our grandmother make her own choices, even those that weren't beneficial to her. She still had Tía Melania and Tío Ramón, but neither of them was clamoring to take her in.

"I've always wondered why she never went straight back to Michoacán after Abuelo died," I said.

But I knew the answer. At her age and in her condition, who of the many relatives she had not seen in decades would take her in? She was more of a stranger there after being away for too long. That was the compromise of migration to the U.S.—it gave a person a different life but at the cost of surrendering the old one. There was no fitting back into the place that had been vacated. Besides, she had become dependent on her pension and medication.

During my visits, Abuela would not take much notice of me, except when she saw that I was alone. She would call me over to the chain-link fence that separated the two properties. Lupe had planted a vine that was steadily crawling up the fence, soon to serve as a shield against her neighbor's critical eyes.

"Estuchi," she said. "I have to tell you something."

Her whispering was unnecessary since there was no one else around. Still, I leaned in. She proceeded to repeat the accusations against Alex and Lupe. I reddened, mortified.

"It's old age, Turrútut," my brother said after I told him. "She's going blind, she's forgetting to take her medication, and she has nothing better to do than snoop and criticize."

On a rare occasion, Tía Melania stopped by to check in on Abuela. Her visits were brief and businesslike, like a military inspection. Abuela would stand there and balk as her daughter threw things out to the back of the house and burned them for whatever reason. If she deemed a dog too sickly and a burden, she had no problems loading it into my uncle's truck, to take it away and abandon it far from Abuela's house. A quick visit to the supermarket to restock the kitchen was followed by a swift good-bye. She was in and out in a matter of hours. That must have suited Abuela just fine since she had become a loner. Despite my brother's assessment, Abuela kept herself busy around the house, watering her plants, cleaning out the bird cages, and relaxing on her front porch with a beer. If anyone called out from the street to greet her, she would grunt a response, if even that. Abuela had become that eccentric old lady on the block that kept to herself, ignoring the world passing her by. Until she found a companion.

Teresita was spotted a few times before Alex and Lupe realized she had moved in. She was slightly younger than Abuela and stronger. In the early morning hours, the washing machine was already running, and the kitchen light was on. As was the music from a small transistor radio she liked to carry with her from one chore to another.

"La señora has a girlfriend," Lupe would joke.

The nature of the relationship was not quite clear, but Teresita's presence there made a huge difference. The garden looked cleaner, the windows were clearer, and what was once unthinkable—bathing the dogs—was taking place right before my brother's eyes. Whatever suspicion Alex had about Teresita's intentions were put at ease for the moment.

"If she ends up with the house," my brother said, "she's earning it."

Teresita didn't talk to the neighbors, likely at Abuela's request, but she did wave once in a while. Her mood was jovial, she whistled and hummed as she went about her daily routine, and she too liked to enjoy a beer on the porch in the afternoon. The chatter was muffled, but the bursts of laughter were a welcome change from the pitiful sight of Abuela sitting sullen and alone.

The portable tray table that had followed Abuela from house to house was cleaned up and propped up so that Abuela could enjoy an afternoon meal outside in the breeze. The finishing touch: Teresita plucked a flower from the garden, stuck it in a glass of water, and then placed it on the corner of the tray. Such attention was unthinkable during our family meals. We were not brought up with any sense of decorum, let alone taught how to appreciate these small details that expressed care and affection.

"Lupe thinks they're girlfriends," Alex reported over the phone. But the statement was made in jest.

I didn't see any of these interactions, but part of me was thrilled by the possibility.

"It doesn't have to be sexual," I said. "Or maybe it is and so what? That's none of our business. The point is she seems happy to be with someone. None of her damn relatives bothered to keep her company."

I was indicting myself as well. I too had abandoned her, more concerned about my own career path and personal life. But unlike her sons, I never came around asking for money or bothered her with my problems. As a grandson, maybe it wasn't my right to do so anyway. When I told people that Abuela had raised me, many responded with "She was a mother to you." That statement didn't feel quite right.

Although my grandmother treated us with care and respect, there was always an emotional distance between us. I always suspected that gender expectations didn't appeal to her. She resisted them as best she could: she could barely cook, she hardly cleaned, and she liked to go out into the fields and work. Domesticity was not her thing, and neither was child-rearing. Yet she had been forced to fulfill this maternal role when her teenage grandsons were dumped at her house. Was it any wonder she embraced solitude like she did? And when she found a wife, she jumped at the opportunity to let her in.

I imagined Teresita was the opposite of Abuela. She moved about like a whirlwind, sweeping the porch, replacing the curtains, beating the dust off the patchwork of rugs Abuelo had placed on the cold concrete floor to protect their feet. She trained the dogs to eat out of old bowls instead of tossing the scraps haphazardly to the ground, which was Abuela's feeding method, and which also incited a fly infestation. But most importantly, Abuela looked refreshed in her clean clothes and nicely coiffed hair.

In the mornings the two women sat outside to sip coffee. Abuela had taken to wearing her costume jewelry once more, and stones glistened as if spit-shined. The steam kept rising from their cups as they talked and laughed, like an old married couple. Suddenly, Teresita got up and walked inside to retrieve her brush—the black one with the flowery design that reminded Abuela of the artisan work from Michoacán. Their conversation continued as Teresita stood behind Abuela, caressing her hair with the brush and then with the palm of her hand. If they weren't talking, then Abuela would close her eyes to listen to Teresita sing a tune from the old days, perhaps one of those somber love songs by Las Jilguerillas: "Amor y lágrimas me han costado en quererte. Amor ingrato, a mi amor has despreciado." (Love and tears your love has cost me. Ungrateful lover, you have despised my love.)

While tending the garden, they remained within whispering distance, as if Teresita was on guard in case Abuela stumbled or complained about a backache. If such a thing happened, Teresita came to the rescue. Within seconds, a chair would appear so that Abuela could sit and rest. Her companion was more than happy to complete any unfinished tasks as long as they were there, together.

At night, did they sleep in the same bed to keep their bodies warm, or did they walk into separate bedrooms? When Abuelo was alive, he and Abuela slept apart. Perhaps Abuelo's snoring became too much after many years. Or perhaps Abuelo tired of Abuela's early mornings and wanted to remain undisturbed until he got hungry enough to leave the comfort of the covers.

Somehow, picturing the women sleeping together made sense. There was so much intimacy expressed in the daytime that it had to spill into the evenings as they sat side by side on the small couch, watching telenovelas until bedtime. What should they have for breakfast the next morning? Abuela

wanted more of her favorite: refried beans and a warm tortilla or two—
no salsa, she was never a fan of anything spicy. Was there any white cheese
left? If not, Teresita would be sure to get some.

"Buenas noches, Mari."

"Buenas noches, Tere."

Or maybe Abuela said goodnight in her language: Náre chúsku. And in
the mornings, Náre erantsku. To speak to someone in your native tongue
was a gesture of respect like no other.

To make the idea that Abuela and Teresita were possibly having a relationship more digestible, I suggested to Alex that perhaps this was a platonic
romance. I was reminded of that talk-show episode with the lesbian couple
and how Abuela had reacted negatively against it. But that was decades ago.
Abuela was in a new place, with a person who didn't mistreat her.

"I mean, they're old women," I said.

"You're probably right," Alex agreed.

My sister-in-law laughed in the background.

"Just because you two can't imagine two old ladies having sex doesn't
mean it's not happening," I heard her say. "You are all the same. Old men—
even older than your grandmother—get to prowl around like dogs in heat.
I mean, look at your Tío Justo. He's going to be a hundred and still embarrassing himself."

The moment became awkward quickly, but Lupe was right. How dare
we deny Abuela her sexuality. When we were younger, Alex and I discovered
a vibrator in the bathroom closet. I thought I had found it first but when
I mentioned it to him, he had already stumbled upon it, digging into the
cubbyhole for a clean towel.

"What do you think?" I asked him. We were only a few years into our
teens.

"Abuelo makes her use it," he concluded.

I didn't mention to Alex that Abuela was somehow adept at ordering
products from the TV, like those face creams, but neither did I ever see
vibrators advertised. It made sense that Abuelo, exercising his perversion,
had bought the sex toy and was forcing it upon her. Abuela, poor innocent
Abuela.

But that was me in my prudish teenage years. I was now a man, decades older, and had seen enough episodes of *The Golden Girls* to know better. It wasn't my business to inquire or to visualize, but to appreciate that this intimacy between two mature women was possible, and welcomed. Besides, it opened the door to the possibility that if Abuela was queer, I would be more connected to her than ever before.

In any case, we concluded that Teresita was a godsend, the reprieve we all wanted in order to excuse ourselves of any responsibility and guilt. How grotesque that the woman who had been forced to raise children and grandchildren was not receiving the attention that she had given us. Thankfully, someone had arrived to serve that need.

It wasn't resentment that had made Abuela cut us off in the first place. I never witnessed a single act that demonstrated she was capable of it. Neither did I ever hear her wish anyone ill-will. If she had any negative thoughts, she kept them to herself, unlike Abuelo, who felt obligated to make these complaints as public as possible, hand gestures and everything.

My brother speculated that she was simply tired of dealing with our shit, especially Abuelo's. After his death, she simply wanted her space back. I related to that. I knew that we all felt suffocated, but very few of us could make our way out. I did, and I made everything possible not to return.

One of my greatest regrets is that I didn't take up the cause of taking Abuela back to Michoacán for a visit since my schedule as a college professor was flexible, and I had the spending money. But I had extricated myself from the family, reducing my interactions to a single weekly phone call with Alex. The only way I managed to forgive myself was by believing that Abuela and I understood each other's self-isolation. I too wanted to get away from everyone; their voices threatened to keep me anchored to a past life I was no longer interested in remembering. Abuela and I simply wanted to breathe.

The only thing I could do was imagine what such a trip would have been like.

Abuela only flew once in her life, to get to my mother's funeral in time, and that was enough. Instead, we would travel by bus, albeit first class, with a working air conditioner and a clean bathroom. Such amenities would be necessary because we would be traveling in the summer. The small TVs hanging from the roof would play a silly comedy or an old black-and-white film starring Pedro Infante or Jorge Negrete—any of their popular movies in which they played lovestruck blue-collar workers who sang like honey in order to woo the blonde beauty, daughter of a wealthy landowner or politician. A movie played every few hours, with plenty of time in between for naps, conversation, or for staring out the window at the deserts of the northern states, the ocean view of the western states, and the mountainous roads in the center of the country.

This was the first time Abuela and I traveled together, just the two of us, and I would be overly protective. I would help her off the bus at rest stops so that she could get some fresh air and move her legs. The roadside eateries were packed with passengers from other buses, but I would manage to find us seats, keeping an eye on the bus because we would both be afraid of getting left behind.

I would order bottled water, even though I would encourage Abuela to indulge in a beer.

"Not yet," she would say. "Once I set foot in my land, I will celebrate."

We would both be hungry, but we were also nervous travelers. We would order something light from the menu: a bowl of chicken soup with warm tortillas for her, and a plate of enchiladas for me. We would consume only half our meals, pay the waitress, and then be the first ones on the bus, anxious until we were back on the road again. This scene would repeat itself again during dinnertime. And twice more the next day.

If I had packed books with me, I wouldn't get to read them. It was much easier to stare at the small TV screen or doze off, striking my head against the window a few times before I surrendered to sleep. Each time I woke up, Abuela would be sitting there, open-eyed.

"Did you get to sleep, Abuela?" I would ask her, and she would say yes, although I suspected she was only taking short naps. The seats were comfortable, but after a day on the road they lost their charm.

When the bus stopped to gas up, the vendors would descend with their tin platters of fruit or juice. Abuela would buy potato chips—those that were cut up and deep fried on the street. This was to be an early taste of things to come. I would decide to follow suit and buy a Jarritos, those Mexican sodas with uncommon flavors: tamarind, watermelon, grapefruit, mandarin, guava. I would be disappointed when the vendor opened the bottle and instead of handing it to me, he would pour the soda in a plastic bag and stick a straw in it. That's how it was done in México, and we were in México now.

It would dawn on me then that even though we were both headed to Zacapu, we would not be staying in the same house. Abuela would go to Tía Juana's house. I would go to Abuelo Melecio and Abuela Herminia's. Where and how would we part ways? At the bus station? I would put Abuela in a taxi and I would insist on walking, which was a kind of ceremony for me. Or I would have to locate a pay phone and have someone from Tía Juana's come pick her up. But not before a meal at el mercado. Abuela would have her beer there to accompany a plate of chicken with rice. I would order the same, and ask for a Jarritos, "sabor de tamarindo," if only to drink it out of the bottle. And afterward, where would we wait? The obvious choice was the town square within view of la Parroquia de Santa Ana. We might decide to sit there for a moment or two, to soak up the afternoon with complete freedom, hoping not to be recognized by members of either side of the family. Not yet.

If we arrived on a weekend, the square would be busy. A band might be setting up in the kiosk. The vendors would be polishing the glass display case of gelatins or churros or donuts. An old woman would likely claim one of the corners for her brazero and oversized comal that toasted peanuts, garbanzo seeds, and sunflower seeds. The old movie theater on Avenida Madero was still there, though slightly updated. But that had to be the same popcorn seller I remembered from my youth. Theatergoers either bought popcorn at the door or made a stop at the old woman's comal. The garbanzos were going fast.

But if it was a weekday, the evening would be quiet. The square would be overrun with schoolchildren getting into one mischief or another, but to them, all the grownups around them were invisible. Young couples leaned against the trees as they caressed. The old men gathered around the shoeshine stations to joke around or debate the latest political scandal.

"There are too many cars now," Abuela would exclaim. How long since the last time she was home? Perhaps those trips we made in Abuelo's truck. They continued to take them each summer even after I had left for college. Eventually Abuelo got tired of the long drive and they simply stayed home. It had to have been 1992, the year they decided to move from California to Mexicali. When Abuela died, she had not been home for almost twenty years.

But the heavier traffic was a small change. Everything else seemed to have frozen in time. It was we who had changed. Abuela had come back a widow. I was still the orphan, but now middle-aged. It didn't matter that Zacapu didn't recognize or remember us. We remembered home quite well. And maybe Abuela would decide to stay for the rest of her days. Maybe it was here that she died, in the company of her younger sister, since Guadalupe, the youngest, had already passed.

But the truth of Abuela's death was unkind. Once Tía Melania found out that a stranger had moved in with Abuela, she thought the worst. Surely someone was taking advantage of her, maybe even stealing her money right under her nose. Enough was enough. It was clear Abuela couldn't look after herself. She would have to return to California and live with her. And if Tía Melania got wind of anything inappropriate taking place in that house, she would be scandalized. Or maybe she did hear the rumors, which is why she flew into action.

That day unfolded quickly. A surprise visit followed by an eviction. Teresita had to gather her things in a matter of minutes under the watchful eye of Tía Melania, just in case the unwanted guest felt the urge to pilfer something on her way out. This was an unkind gesture because Abuela had no valuables. To guard the knickknacks and the knockoffs was a way to humiliate the suspected thief, to let her know that she was of little consequence herself.

I imagine Abuela became enraged, but her soft voice hardly registered this. She might have grabbed Teresita's arm, like a child holding on stubbornly to something that was being taken away. Tía Melania, the figure of authority present, was stronger and had no trouble unlocking Abuela's hand from Teresita. Teresita must have been inconsolable, looking back at her companion's helplessness, but saddened even more by the knowledge that Abuela would blame herself for not fighting harder.

Gone was the small talk in the mornings and Teresita's gentle reminders to take her pills. Gone was the rhythm of the broom as Teresita swept the floor. There would be no more gasping at the antics of the telenovela villains or bursts of laughter at the outlandish skits with those aging comedians who looked worse for wear but who still performed physical gags. Good-bye, hairbrush. Good-bye, Jilguerillas. Good-bye, happiness. And love, good-bye, good-bye.

"Te quiero, María," Teresita might have called out. And that made everyone witnessing this drama freeze, including Tía Melania, who looked befuddled all of a sudden. She quickly shook it off and shooed Teresita off the property, but not before Abuela shouted an I love you back, but in her tongue: "Jikeni kánekua tsïpesïnga exeni."

And then Abuela went quiet, but her silence was resignation as she watched Teresita wander off as suddenly as she had wandered in, with a bag of belongings and a jaunt that seemed too upbeat for the occasion.

Had any one of us ever told Abuela María that we loved her? We didn't express such sentimental thoughts in the González family. Who had time for love when there was rent, and medical expenses, and another child on the way?

That day, Abuela lost her dogs, her house, and her companion. Not long after, she died. Not only did she die away from her homeland, but away from the space she called her own, a tiny paradise where she could rise whenever she wanted, eat whatever she wanted, and do whatever she wanted.

"That's the end of a generation," people say when the last of the elders passes on. But more than the generation is lost. Also, the stories, the memories, and the ties to the recent past. With Abuela's death, the answers to our questions also died. I never got to ask her about how she crossed the border. Nor why she made that decision to migrate to the U.S. with Abuelo back in the 1960s. What kept them in this country all this time? What kept her in that marriage? And what did Teresita mean to her?

I recall our summer treks down to Michoacán in Abuelo's truck, when we usually made a stop in Nahuatzen, Abuela's hometown. Our stay was so brief that sometimes Abuela and I didn't even have a chance to stretch our legs. I never understood the meaning of this gesture, and that is one more mystery I will not have a chance to ask about. But on one occasion, Abuela did step out of the truck, and seconds later someone recognized her.

"María!" the woman called out and rushed over to hug Abuela.

I was more impressed by the fact that they spoke to each other in Purépecha but peppered with Spanish. It was a quick conversation because soon after Abuelo came back and smiled apologetically as he pulled Abuela away from this acquaintance, who might have been a relative or an old friend. The woman knew exactly what was happening in front of her and didn't hide her displeasure.

Later that afternoon, we arrived at Tía Sara's house, where Abuelo insisted we remain instead of seeking out members of the other side of the family, meaning my maternal grandparents and Abuela's siblings. Even Tía Sara took pity on us for being caged in like that and encouraged us to sneak out. She wouldn't tell. She promised.

Abuela walked into my designated bedroom that evening to bring me a cup of tea made with leaves from the orange tree. She had put plenty of sugar in it, which is how she liked it, but I drank it anyway.

"Abuela," I said. "What is it that you and that lady talked about in Nahuatzen?"

She laughed. "Tolondrones pa' los preguntones," she said.

I chuckled. That was Mamá Lola's favorite phrase. A response to a question she didn't want to answer. Knocks on the head for the nosy. Meaning, none of your business, but said in a benevolent way. I let it go, even though I knew that if she had told me, I would have gained some insight into this strained dynamic between her and Abuelo.

Without Abuela, her house also lost its will to live. The roof began to waste away, and the garden dried up. The large birdcage Abuela kept in the yard was now empty, and once in a while a wild bird swooped down to pick at the seeds of the abandoned feeder.

"What happened to the dogs?" I asked my brother.

"I don't know. They either took them to the pound or threw them away somewhere in the desert."

Weeks after the incident, a stray dog came sniffing around. My brother didn't really pay attention to the dogs next door. He wasn't sure if this was one of Abuela's pets that had somehow found its way back or if it was just another street animal that had caught the scent of the dogs now missing.

"It just stood there, you know," Alex said. "Just staring toward the house as if it had some connection to it. Maybe it was remembering its past. Or maybe it was seeing ghosts."

I wanted to tell my brother that those two things were the same. Seeing ghosts was all we had now that most of the older members of the González family were dead.

"Have you noticed Teresita coming around? Whatever happened to her?"

Alex paused, as if he was thinking about it for the first time.

"You know, she was there such a short time, it's as if I dreamed the whole thing. I don't even remember what she looks like. I'm not even sure of her name anymore."

"It wasn't Teresita?"

"Maybe. Or something that sounded like Teresita. Margarita. Carmelita. Something like that. Does it matter? She came and went and that's it."

And poof! Just like that, Teresita—or whatever her name was—vanished all over again. But, like that woman on the streets of Nahuatzen, she had with her a precious piece of Abuela that was not offered to any of us left behind because we had not been entitled to it. María Carrillo was her own person. She didn't belong to us.

Fieldwork

Amarillo. Yellow, like the sun. Tsipampiti. Y para decir sol se dice jurhiáta.

—Abuela's lessons in Purépecha

IN MAY 1993, I had just completed my first year in the MA program at UC–Davis. Since the department did not provide summer funding, most of the graduate students scrambled to find ways to make ends meet. One person announced with dismay that they would be bartending, another bemoaned her return to waitressing, and still another scoffed at the idea of standing behind a cash register all day, dealing with high-maintenance clients. They were all caught off guard, however, when I shared my employment plans: I was joining my family in the grape fields.

At the time, my brother, my father, and Tío Rafa were all living in El Rancho. Alex informed me that they had been driving up from Mexicali to the Coachella Valley and rented a small one-room apartment with a few other men. Such communal arrangements were common during the harvesting season. My grandparents still lived in El Campo but were getting their affairs in order because they too planned to move to El Rancho to live out their retirement. Abuela had wanted to work one last time in the fields, a desire Abuelo made no objection to since it would be useful to have additional funds in preparation for the move. The only way I could spend time with Alex and Abuela during my visit was to sign up for this early morning trek to the vineyards in the desert.

There was a second, more self-serving reason for my willingness to suffer through long hours of heat and dehydration: I wanted to write a book about the grape pickers. I flew down to Southern California, prepared to ask questions, take notes, and even snap pictures with a small disposable camera I bought at the local pharmacy. I told my friends at the university, tongue in cheek, that I was conducting "field research."

The gravity of my choice sunk in on my first day on the job. Abuela woke me up at 5 a.m. I changed into clothes that I would have to toss out at the end of the season because by then they were going to be grape-stained and saturated in sulfur. After splashing some water on my face, I joined Abuela at the dining table for a cup of coffee. Our cue to walk out the door would be my father honking the horn as he drove up.

"I forgot what a pain in the ass it is to get up at this hour," I informed Abuela.

Abuela chuckled, adjusting the bandanna wrapped around her head. "Just wait until quitting time."

I marveled at how, at sixty-four, Abuela appeared eager to head to the grape fields. She had been doing this type of labor since the 1960s, long before I was born.

"Aren't you glad this is the last time you'll be out in the burning sun?" I asked. The apartment was quiet. We could hear Abuelo's heavy breathing as he slept. He had filed for disability years prior. Since then, he stayed home year-round preparing the meals while Abuela endured long hours at the packinghouses or in the grape fields. It took two years to convince her to retire.

"I don't know," she said.

I didn't want to press her further. I couldn't imagine there was much joy in the labor, but this was the world she had been living in most of her life. Abuelo certainly wasn't a fan of agricultural work. When his disability case was approved, we all thought his grouchiness and mood swings would taper down, but the luxury of staying home to nap while everyone else was out of the house encouraged very little change.

The honk outside got us moving. Our harvesting scissors and lunch were in Abuela's bag, which I carried out to the car as I put on a baseball cap. I joined Alex and my uncle in the back seat.

Of course, we were one of the first vehicles to arrive. This was a habit my family couldn't break, and which drove Alex and me crazy because it made no sense to us that we got there early only to wait another thirty minutes to an hour before starting time. Abuelo claimed it was to secure a good parking spot, but when I adopted the same practice as a professor, I realized that this was insurance against arriving late. Anything could happen on the way, and the last thing we wanted was to jeopardize our reputation for punctuality.

The morning was cool. As more people arrived, the banter and pleasantries were punctuated by the occasional burst of laughter. For them it was the middle of the grape-picking season. They had already built friendships and bonds. I took the opportunity to separate myself from the group to take a few pictures of the vineyard. The panorama was quite lovely and serene. The light was slowly creeping over the mountain range. In a matter of hours, the heat would intensify, eventually reaching temperatures close to one hundred degrees by noon. After the supervisor blew his whistle, everyone took their places in the rows of grapevines.

Since we were a unit of five, we took two rows. Alex and my father took one. Abuela and I took another. Tío Rafa was our packer. He set up his table and umbrella. I carried Abuela's box to the end of the row. We each had to carry the boxes back to my uncle as we filled them with bunches of grapes. But we agreed to take turns carrying Abuela's.

"You're fucking crazy, Turrútut," Alex said.

I laughed. "Maybe I like to suffer."

"You sure do. You left this life, why the hell did you come back?"

The soil was soft and deep. At the moment it was only a nuisance to pull my feet out, but once the day became hotter, the warmth would make my feet sweat. All the burdens of grape picking were becoming clear again.

Abuela usually kept quiet. She was a much faster grape picker than the rest of us, but when I took my uncle her first box, he shook his head.

"My poor mother," he said. "Decades in the field and she never learned how to pick properly."

Lunch hour was at 9 a.m., three hours after starting time. Quitting time could be anywhere between noon and 2 p.m., depending on the heat. It wasn't good to harvest when the grape was too hot. I made mental notes of all these details, expecting to transfer them to my notebook back at the apartment.

The mood during mealtime was similar to the period of arrival, a laugh or a chuckle here and there. Abuela opened up the bag to distribute the bean burritos while my father cleared our lunch spot of the grapevines. We kneeled to eat except for Abuela, who sat down on the mound of soil around the grape trunk.

"Is it all too familiar?" my father joked.

I nodded. I was famished. But the meal was light. Tío Rafa passed around the orange water cooler and a single plastic cup.

"I'm going to put all this in a book someday," I said.

My statement was met with silence, but I didn't expect any particular response. Abuela only wrote her name. My father and uncle didn't get past elementary school. My brother had dropped out of high school. I was the college boy who had traded the library for the fields, an act that must have come across as frivolous. I was supposed to be studying to be a teacher. That's how I explained it to them. This book idea probably came across as a passing interest, one more way to exercise all the extra schooling I had signed up for.

"I even brought a camera to take a picture or two," I said. I reached into Abuela's bag.

"Just don't let the supervisor catch you," my father warned me. He and my uncle didn't wear protective gear on their heads.

A whistle blew. We cleared the area. Abuela and I resumed our places, opposite each other. My father and Tío Rafa switched roles.

"I wish your brother had stayed in school," she said. "Now he's stuck doing this line of work."

Abuela's voice was soft. I didn't worry about Alex hearing us. Besides, Tío Rafa was more talkative than my father, but I couldn't make out his chatter.

"He just turned twenty-one," I said. "He can probably find other options."

I didn't want to worry Abuela with the fact that Alex had expressed his desire to bartend.

"I'm glad you made your way to something different," she said. "But don't come back here again."

I couldn't help but feel that she was referring to more than the fields. Or maybe I was projecting. I'm the one who had escaped, who had left five years ago with no intention of ever coming back. This summer project was a last hurrah. One final reminder of why I had torn myself away from the Coachella Valley.

Abuela walked slowly, but her grape-picking method was frantic. She pulled one bunch from the vine, the stem between two fingers, cut it loose, and then instead of dropping that bunch into the box she grabbed another, the stem between two other fingers and so on. Not until she had gathered three or four bunches, depending on the size of the cluster, did she let them go. I was less efficient, cutting each bunch from the vine and then gently placing it on the box because I didn't want to damage it. We were expected to preserve the table grape's aesthetic value. Otherwise they wouldn't be attractive enough to sell at the market.

When Abuela filled her box, she started filling mine, which was my cue to take hers to the packer and then grab an empty box on the way back. I lifted the box and felt a sharp pain on my back.

"Ay, güey," I said. Abuela started laughing.

This wasn't the only agricultural labor Abuela had done in her thirty-plus years of working in the fields. She had also uprooted cabbage and onion. She had climbed on ladders to pluck lemons, oranges, and grapefruit. And when she wasn't sweating outdoors, she was standing for hours behind the packinghouse conveyor belts, sorting dates, carrots, and ears of corn. We knew what she was sorting because she snuck out a few choice pieces, which looked nothing like the wimpy fruit that was sold in our local markets. The corn and the carrots made their way into Abuelo's stews. The dates we would have for dessert.

When I got to the end of the row, I circled around the stack of packed boxes, which had reached my eye level. My father surprised me by standing at the packing table with the disposable camera aimed at me. After he snapped the picture, he quickly put the camera back into Abuela's bag.

"What was that for?" I asked, amused.

"So that you never forget," he said.

He took the box from me. "Ay, güey," he said. "Tell your grandmother not to overfill these boxes. She's going to crush the grapes."

I walked back to my spot and dropped the box under the vines. I didn't mention to Abuela what my father had said because I knew she wouldn't listen.

"And in this book that you're going to write, am I going to be in it?" Tío Rafa's voice cut through the vines. I heard the leaves ruffling as he moved them to pick grapes, but I couldn't make him out.

I laughed. "Maybe," I said.

"If you do, don't mention your Tía Marta," he said. "Say that I was always a bachelor and that I had tons of girlfriends. Right, Alex?"

Alex and I just chuckled. Tío Rafa and Tía Marta had divorced not long ago. The first legal separation I had heard of in our family. She had remarried and moved with her three children to Bakersfield. I was in contact with one of my cousins and had made plans to visit them because it was an easy train ride from Davis to Bakersfield, which just happened to be the city where Alex and I were born. I shared none of this with anyone here.

When I turned around to face Abuela again, she looked sad. With my uncle's divorce, she had lost three of her youngest grandchildren.

"Can I get you some water, Abuela?" I said, trying to distract her.

"Not yet," she said. She reached up to fix her bandanna. "I'm going to have to get a hat."

"Do you want mine?" I offered.

"No, that's fine," she said. "You have to protect that brain of yours. You're still a schoolboy."

"Abuela," I said. "I hope one day I can take you with me."

I surprised myself with this sentimental admission. Take her how? To where? I was only a graduate student, with a silly dream to become a writer. I couldn't imagine how I was going to support myself, let alone another person. I wanted to pull those words back into my mouth because I didn't know how to make that wish come true.

"Ay, Tuchi," she said. "Don't worry about me anymore. You worry about yourself and your future. Don't end up like your cousins, getting involved with drugs or women who can't even make a pot of beans. Marry a good girl like Vikki and give thanks to God you didn't end up working like an animal like the rest of us."

My mouth dried up. That picture she was painting of my future looked foreign. I had become more public about my sexuality because I felt safer away from the Coachella Valley. I had kicked the crystal meth habit I picked up as an undergraduate in Riverside but had picked up heavy drinking in Davis. After a few embarrassing incidents at parties, I was asked to consider seeing a therapist and joining Alcoholics Anonymous. The Big Book remained stored and unread in my desk drawer. I had indeed escaped home to become someone else, and I wasn't happy about it.

As the weeks passed by, we settled into our routines. I was too exhausted to think about the book I was writing and only on occasion did I remember to note something down, mostly character sketches of the people I came across in the fields. There was the supervisor with his high-pitched voice because he had a bullet embedded in his throat that could not be removed without damaging his vocal cords. There was the other female senior in the crew, a tiny woman who clashed often with the supervisor and who threatened to tell her son who was a sheriff. And then there was that young man who looked bitter and resentful. His father badgered him in front of everyone until he lashed out and threatened to join the army. The whole crew stood still until the supervisor broke the tension by saying, "You do that at home!" The young man didn't return to the fields after that. This world that I was leaving behind was rich and complex but troubling.

The plan to spend quality time with my family didn't quite work out. On the weekends, Alex, my father, and my uncle drove back to Mexicali to reunite with their respective significant others. Abuelo and Abuela had gotten used to my presence rather quickly, and they slipped back into the way it used to be when it was just us three: they, fixed to the TV in the living room; me, fading in the background as night fell.

My silver lining was that without those college parties, I had no desire to drink. I drank because I felt out of place, isolated, and lonely. Because I missed a family I never had. Coming back was a reminder that I had made it out. I didn't exit intact, and I remained broken in some ways. Still, I resolved to keep myself sober. I was afraid I would end up like my father, who was a funny drunk in public but a somber one in private. He burned through his money and then begged my brother and me for more. When we denied him, he sunk deeper into depression because his sons had abandoned him.

"How's his drinking?" I asked my brother discreetly.

Alex shook his head. "He keeps himself in check while he's here, but you should see him when he gets back to Mexicali. He parks it on the front porch and surrounds himself with bottles of beer."

I didn't have to work hard to imagine that sight because I had seen it on a number of occasions. My father sat on the ground, leaning against the wall of the house, the beer bottles clustered about like pets he was about to feed. When he was intoxicated enough, his mischievous children tossed pebbles from a distance. Sometimes they struck their target and the bottles would clink. A celebratory outburst followed. Other times the pebbles struck my father, and he would swat theatrically as if he were fighting a bee. That made his children giggle. The game continued until his second wife, Amelia, pulled him up by his shirt collar and walked him inside the house.

As the harvesting season wound down, our exchanges across the vines were reduced to polite chit-chat, nothing inspired enough to record in my notebook. It didn't occur to me that I should be writing down whatever family tidbits I picked up from Tío Rafa, my father, or Abuela, because I didn't imagine myself writing about them. I wrote poetry and fiction. Nonfiction was too hurtful to attempt. Instead, I had gathered snippets of conversations I picked up as I eavesdropped on the farmworkers who were strangers, and descriptions of the farmworkers themselves. These notes would suffice to motivate this novel idea I had about a crew of grape pickers. It was much safer to shape the world of make-believe than to confront the realities that still haunted me.

After weeks in the sun, our bodies had grown weary. I became especially frustrated at my father's propensity to socialize during quitting time, when all I wanted was to get home and rinse out the dirt and sulfur in my ears.

I had been wearing the same pair of jeans, now juice-stained, and long-sleeved cotton shirt that had grown thin from Abuela's daily washings. I was relieved when I heard that we would stop working any day now. Our crew had already connected with another in the same vineyard—a sure sign that the Coachella Valley harvest was nearing its completion.

Freshly bathed and with a thick layer of moisturizer on my face, I sat on the same living room couch that had been my bed through most of high school. Abuela was outside doing the laundry. In the kitchen, Abuelo banged the stirring spoon against the pot.

"The rice is almost warm again," he said.

I had grown to enjoy Abuelo's cooking. He rarely prepared traditional Mexican meals. He preferred Asian cuisine, particularly Chinese and Filipino. The scent of boiled bitter melon was so familiar to me that when I smelled it in other places, it always reminded me of home.

Abuelo placed the rice and a heaping plate of vermicelli noodles and vegetables on the table.

"Eat," he commanded. He brought down the loaf of white bread, though I had given up bread as an undergraduate when I found out Asian people didn't combine rice and bread like this.

"Rice provides the carbs already," my then-girlfriend Vikki had explained.

I picked up the fork. I would be eating alone because Abuelo fed himself by the time we arrived from work and Abuela liked to eat much later in the afternoon. Even when we didn't have these schedules, we rarely sat down at the table as a family. I was surprised when Abuelo sat down across from me to observe.

"Do you eat like this up there?" he asked.

His question reminded me of that time he asked us, while we were in middle school, what kind of food was served in the cafeteria. Alex looked at me, uncertainly. Since I skipped lunch to read in the library, he had to answer.

"Spaghetti and meatballs," he said.

"Meatballs," Abuelo said. "I can make those. What else?"

"French fries," Alex said.

"I make those all the time, you know that," Abuelo said. And then he explained himself: "I heard there was a job opening for a cook. I think I might go see what it's all about."

Later, in the privacy of our room, Alex scoffed. "Yeah, right," he said. "Can you imagine Abuelo making those Mexican meatballs with those worms sticking out of them?"

"They're not worms, they're grains of rice. And I like them," I said.

"And french fries. He calls his greasy potatoes french fries? He's going to give all the kids diarrhea!"

We never did find out if Abuelo showed up at Woodrow Wilson Middle School to inquire about the position, but it made me sad still that the people hiring might have laughed at Abuelo's lack of knowledge about American cafeterias. But also, it signaled to me that Abuelo too wanted to follow another path.

I swallowed a big bite of rice soaked in bitter melon juice. "I lived in a dormitory last year. Meals were included," I said to Abuelo. "This year I'm moving into a house with roommates. None of us know how to cook, but there are many restaurants around because it's a college town."

"Restaurant food is not very tasty," he said. "And it's expensive."

I didn't want to contradict him. There were plenty of cheap eats for the college student budget. And I had no qualms about the taste.

"You know, Estuche," he said. Since he had used the nickname Abuela had given me, I knew there was something big coming.

"If you want," he continued, "we could move up there with you instead of moving to Mexicali. Abuela could do the cleaning and I could do the cooking. It would be a good arrangement for all of us."

I felt light-headed. The suggestion was too great for me to process. I wondered if Abuela had told him that I had expressed my desire to take her with me someday. Abuelo had latched on to that possibility and made it his. I should have been specific with Abuela. That I had meant take her *away* from Abuelo someday, where she could do and say whatever she wanted without having to contend with his mood swings. That I wanted her to escape this man's grasp the way I had.

"I don't know," I said to Abuelo. "I don't have my own place yet, and I'm only there for another year. Who knows where I'll be after that."

"We can follow you anywhere," Abuelo said. "What do we own? A beat-up old truck with a crooked camper and this console TV that's got a few years left to live. I should have put it out of its misery a long time ago."

The moment had become awkward. I lost my appetite, yet I stared down at my plate. Abuelo must have sensed this also. He got up and gave me a pat on the back.

"Well, you think about it," he said. "You just say the word and we'll be there."

I never did say the word. Eventually, they moved to Mexicali, taking their clunky console TV with them, and I moved to Arizona, then New Mexico, then New York City, farther and farther until I was so distant that the news of their deaths arrived long after the funerals. The only thing I had taken with me from that summer was the pictures I took in the fields. I lost track of all of them, except for the one my father took of me carrying a box of grapes. I was smiling stupidly, as if I didn't have a care in the world. I framed the photograph and have placed it on every writing desk I've ever had, a reminder of the past, and how far I have traveled from the grape fields, the Coachella Valley, and Abuelo.

That afternoon, my father made an unexpected visit. Tío Rafa and Alex were with him. They came with the news that the grape harvest was over, and that they were leaving for Mexicali, not to return again until asparagus season. Final paychecks would be available the following week. One of them would come back to claim them.

"How does it feel?" my father asked me.

"Good," I said, though I was unprepared for this sudden transition.

I was relieved, but this abrupt end was anticlimactic, with no good-bye party or celebration. What had brought us together had concluded. Now everyone could go back to their respective households.

Tío Rafa didn't want to waste any more time. His new girlfriend was waiting for him and he looked forward to chasing her around the house as she tried to avoid his tickling hands.

"I don't stop until she farts," he said.

Abuelo let out a burst of laughter.

There was no hugging or hand-shaking. The Gonzálezes were as unsentimental about their farewells as they were about their hellos. As I watched them prepare to leave, I felt as if my body was a tub of water that had sprung a leak and was quickly emptying. I followed my brother out the door and watched him climb into the car.

"Later, Turrútut," Alex said. And off they went.

Abuela didn't react to any of it. She leaned back on the couch to enjoy her beer, letting out a self-satisfied belch. Abuelo bent down to turn the TV volume up and then sat next to her.

I felt out of place again. I had to start planning my own departure. It would have to be a weekend, so that my friend Sandra didn't have to leave work early to pick me up at the Greyhound Station. Booking an airline ticket back to Northern California took one brief phone call. How easy it was to leave. It was the coming back home that was becoming difficult.

Abuelo and Abuela postponed their move to Mexicali one more year. I had bought a car from a friend in the Bay Area, and my father flew up to help me drive back to the Coachella Valley. I would drive solo the rest of the way to Tempe, Arizona, where I would work toward a second graduate degree.

"More school," Abuelo quipped. "What else is there to learn?"

Abuela saw me off then too. I rose at the crack of dawn because I had heard Arizona was even hotter than the Coachella Valley in the summer, and I didn't want to overheat the old Celica and get stuck in an unfamiliar place with strange people who might not be compelled to help a stranded newcomer. I drank the last cup of coffee Abuela would ever make for me. I ate the last plate of fried eggs and beans she would ever cook for me. We were silent because Abuelo was asleep in the bedroom, though we knew our soft voices would not wake him. Still, we didn't say much, attuned to the pending good-bye.

"I'm leaving now," I said.

Abuela cried, blessing me with the sign of the cross. I started sobbing and couldn't stop as I climbed into the car, started the engine, and backed out of the parking spot. I had begun this independent journey long ago. I was not turning back.

As I drove off, I prayed that one day I would be able to bring Abuela with me, take her away from all this.

And then, suddenly, I found myself standing over her grave.

And then, suddenly, the news came by way of a friend who still lived in the Coachella Valley that El Campo was getting torn down. I informed my brother, who responded, incredulously, "Really?"

Yes, really. We had even outlived El Campo.

Our California childhood was a pile of dust. There would be no evidence left of our time there. Razed, El Campo would look as flat as the field of graves in the Coachella Valley Public Cemetery. New housing would be built on top of it, just like the high-rise graves of el Panteón San Franciscano.

When I was younger, I would hear the older folks say, "Enjoy your youth because the years go by fast." But when one is young, stretching out the hours doing the most mundane of things, it feels as if there is all the time in the world. Until time actually does run out. For me, that meant contending with the unresolved narratives after getting left behind by my loved ones who pass away. The three deaths I have had to process were my father's, Abuelo's, and Abuela's. My relationships with my father and Abuelo, however, are full of conflict and heartbreak, and those tensions have allowed me to reflect, at least, on what happened and why. But my memories of Abuela are not buoyed by rage or even by what some might call love. Abuela was simply there, a witness on the sidelines. And I deliberately forgot about her because I couldn't remember her outside those troubling years of my life. That's the real travesty in all of this. When I had access to her, I didn't ask any questions because the house was noisy with anger and violence. After I broke away, I still didn't make an effort to get to know her. I was too preoccupied by then, sorting out my wonky journey through adulthood. Now that I was finally interested in knowing more, the roads back to her had been erased by time but also by neglect and disinterest.

On one of those weekly phone calls with my brother, I said solemnly, "I wish I knew more about Abuela to write about."

"How well do we know anyone in the family, dude?" he said. "We left when we were young and didn't care to go back."

I suppose that's the letdown of trying to recall the past. I strayed far. Everything I saw looked much smaller, fuzzier, and turned away from me. Yet the hurt was as large as ever.

I offer my own language lesson for solace. Here, Americans say to fly. Mexicans say volar. In Purépecha it's kárani. Here, Americans say to write. Mexicans say escribir. In Purépecha it's karáni. The words kárani and karáni sound almost identical. Perhaps because they are the same in that to write is to imagine, and so is to fly. I have to imagine in order to outpace forgetting and to fill in the absences in the narratives.

I've written down what I know. The only thing I have left in my hand is the promise that I will, sooner or later, take Abuela's ashes to Michoacán.

The next time I spoke with my friend Sandra in California, we made plans for our fifty-first birthdays. Our fiftieth was a wash since it took place in the middle of the pandemic of 2020. That awkward Zoom birthday party was a weak substitute for the cruise around the Greek islands we had planned. As middle-aged professionals with spending money our families never thought possible, we were making the best of it since neither of us was married or had children.

"Familylessness has its privileges," I quipped, though the word felt sour in the mouth.

"We can have fun at home if it's still not safe enough to travel," she suggested. "We can go to the beach, or to the Getty Museum. We can drive to Old Town in San Diego, maybe go hiking in Yosemite Park. There's a lot to do and no one to stop us."

"I have a request, though," I said.

"What is it?"

"I want us to go to the cemetery in the Coachella Valley. You can take flowers to your father and I can take flowers to my grandmother."

"We can do that," she said. "We can visit my mom and you can pick up some dates from her tree. You're always complaining how dry and expensive they are on the East Coast."

"That will be lovely," I said.

After a brief silence, Sandra said, "Hey, did you get far with that book about your grandma?"

"That's the funny thing," I said. "All this time I thought she was a light in my past. But I've come to realize that she's actually mostly shadow."

"To you," Sandra said.

"What?"

"She's mostly shadow to you. But I bet you that's not how she saw herself."

I took comfort in that statement. It didn't excuse the choice that I had made to go away and stay away, even from Abuela. But it made my short-comings on this journey of rediscovery that much less inconsequential. To her story anyway. I had what I had. She kept the rest of it. And what an extraordinary ownership that must have been. No, María Carrillo was not missing. She was, and will always be, mostly out of my line of sight.

Acknowledgments

Sections of this memoir appear in *Between Certain Death and a Possible Future: Queer Writing on Growing Up with the AIDS Crisis* (Arsenal Pulp Press, 2021), edited by Mattilda B. Sycamore; *Contra Viento*; *Good River Review*; *Hostos Review / Revista Hostosiana*; and *Nepantla Familias: An Anthology of Mexican-American Literature of Families in between Worlds* (Texas A&M Press, 2021), edited by Sergio Troncoso. This book was made possible by a 2020 grant from the New Jersey Council for the Arts and a 2020 Lannan Literary Fellowship. Many thanks to my brother, Alex—Turrútut—who jogged my memory during our weekly morning phone calls.

RIGOBERTO GONZÁLEZ is the author of eighteen books of poetry and prose, including the memoir *What Drowns the Flowers in Your Mouth: A Memoir of Brotherhood*, a finalist for the National Book Critics Circle Award. His awards include Lannan, Guggenheim, NEA, NYFA, and USA Rolón fellowships, the PEN/Voelcker Award, the American Book Award from the Before Columbus Foundation, the Lenore Marshall Prize from the Academy of American Poets, and the Shelley Memorial Prize from the Poetry Society of America. A critic-at-large for the *LA Times* and a contributing editor for *Poets & Writers Magazine*, he is the series editor for the Camino del Sol Latinx Literary Series at the University of Arizona Press. Currently, he's Distinguished Professor of English and the director of the MFA Program in Creative Writing at Rutgers-Newark, the State University of New Jersey.

LIVING OUT

Gay and Lesbian Autobiographies

DAVID BERGMAN, JOAN LARKIN, and RAPHAEL KADUSHIN
Founding Editors

In My Father's Arms: A Son's Story of Sexual Abuse
Walter A. de Milly III

Lawfully Wedded Husband: How My Gay Marriage Will Save the American Family
Joel Derfner

Midlife Queer: Autobiography of a Decade, 1971–1981
Martin Duberman

Self-Made Woman: A Memoir
Denise Chanterelle DuBois

The Black Penguin
Andrew Evans

The Man Who Would Marry Susan Sontag: And Other Intimate Literary Portraits of the Bohemian Era
Edward Field

Body, Remember: A Memoir
Kenny Fries

In the Province of the Gods
Kenny Fries

Travels in a Gay Nation: Portraits of LGBTQ Americans
Philip Gambone

Abuela in Shadow, Abuela in Light
Rigoberto González

Autobiography of My Hungers
Rigoberto González

What Drowns the Flowers in Your Mouth: A Memoir of Brotherhood
Rigoberto González

Widescreen Dreams: Growing Up Gay at the Movies
Patrick E. Horrigan

The End of Being Known: A Memoir
Michael Klein

Through the Door of Life: A Jewish Journey between Genders
Joy Ladin

*The Last Deployment: How a Gay, Hammer-Swinging Twentysomething Survived a
    Year in Iraq*
Bronson Lemer

Eminent Maricones: Arenas, Lorca, Puig, and Me
Jaime Manrique

1001 Beds: Performances, Essays, and Travels
Tim Miller

Body Blows: Six Performances
Tim Miller

Cleopatra's Wedding Present: Travels through Syria
Robert Tewdwr Moss

Good Night, Beloved Comrade: The Letters of Denton Welch to Eric Oliver
Edited and with an introduction by Daniel J. Murtaugh

Taboo
Boyer Rickel

Men I've Never Been
Michael Sadowski

Secret Places: My Life in New York and New Guinea
Tobias Schneebaum

Wild Man
Tobias Schneebaum

Sex Talks to Girls: A Memoir
Maureen Seaton